TREGENNA HILL

TREGENNA HILL

ALTARS AND ALLEGORIES

Caitlin Smith Gilson

Foreword by Jennifer Newsome Martin

RESOURCE *Publications* • Eugene, Oregon

TREGENNA HILL
Altars and Allegories

Resource Publications
An Imprint of Wipf and Stock Publishers
199 W. 8th Ave., Suite 3
Eugene, OR 97401

www.wipfandstock.com

PAPERBACK ISBN: 978-1-6667-3203-0
HARDCOVER ISBN: 978-1-6667-2527-8
EBOOK ISBN: 978-1-6667-2528-5

.   NOVEMBER 9, 2021 3:08 PM

For Fred—May time, in its most secret tending, spill over the edge of each day which remains our own and fill your frame with the ecstasy of the love you have given me.

And for the eternal sunshine of our babies, now grown.

TABLE OF CONTENTS

FOREWORD

TREGENNA HILL: ALTARS AND ALLEGORIES includes two discrete cycles of poems, *Tregenna Hill* (twenty poems) and *Summa Solemnis* (four poems): twenty-four poems which are circled around the glorious throne of God like those twenty-four shining elders in the apocalypse of John of Patmos. If the Book of Revelation is among the most sensory of biblical texts— the cacophonous sounds of trumpets blaring, the smell of the smoke of condemned Babylon burning, the taste of scrolls, sweet on the tongue but bitter in the belly, which must nonetheless be eaten, and so on and so forth—this collection of poems likewise involves (even demands!) the attention of the full sensorium. The poems are both sensate and sensual, evoking against all ghosts and specters and haunts of abstraction, images which are relentlessly, defiantly embodied. In "Light of All Valleys, Light of All Faces," the poem goes so far as to declare that "Touch is the forgotten transcendental/Paved over with Roman cobbles/Utterly human and resignedly rare." The reader can almost smell the citrus from a cursed lime tree, the smoke of burning coal, lilacs in bloom, amber perfume, clean soap, warm bread, rotting apples, sacred candles, the salt of sweat, delicate strawberries, earthworms baking in the sun, basil cooked with garlic, the sap of fresh-cut pine, summer thunderstorms, Lenten lilies, honeysuckle; she can taste the mellowed wines, dark chocolate, yeast bread, crepes, black pepper; hear the strains of Bach's *Mass in B Minor*, Ella Fitzgerald's "Those Foolish Things," Handel's operatic *Sona nata lagrimar*. At the aural level, too, the language of Smith Gilson's poetry itself expertly plays with sound, relishing the sheer musical delight of such juxtapositions as "cobble's rabble," "carillon . . . carrion," "shins . . . shining," "Stillness steals," just to name a few instances out of the embarrassment of sonic riches contained herein.

While these marvelously literate poems could be argued to allude to figures as diverse as Homer, Aeschylus, Cervantes, Dostoevsky, Pascal, Nietzsche, Kierkegaard, Heidegger, Eliot, Chesterton, Eugene O'Neill, and Walker Percy, among quite a number of others, there is something else more fundamental of Revelation about them. That is, there is a quality of ecstatic vision which sees all at once, which sees in and across time and its exigencies and sorrows to a final gathering up and gathering into a shape where time shall be no more. Turned toward this final ingathering or infolding into "form," a word that appears across the collection some three dozen times, the speaker writes in the revelatory "Gozo to Patmos," "You alone crack open the form/And can comprehend/The lapsing moment where I am now/A passenger of past perfections." Later, in "In the Cower," the poem's speaker prays: "Bring me back to form . . . Hollow me out and fill me in." Yet even as the poems gesture to an eschatological resolution where this mysterious form will give us back our truest selves, they simultaneously disclose a furious hope laced with something hard like defiance. This holy defiance is aimed squarely at any suggestion that to position oneself toward the futurity of the last things is to expunge or obliterate the past or present, the *then* or the *now*, or the body in preference to the spirit. The eschatological summing up or re-collection of the self in glory, as well as that final summing up of those we've known, held, loved, and lost for the present time must be a phenomenon of restoration which does not circumvent the personal, the particular, the idiosyncratic, the natural, the enfleshed, the rich texture and tapestry of an embodied life.

Though it may well be true that "last things are the only things that last" ("Your Enduring Inelegance") the poems resolutely refuse to capitulate on the insistent fact that "*we* are among the last things that last" ("Let the Waterfalls Fall Over Me"). And "we" are stubborn flesh entangled in stubborn time; we may not forget the *then*, a phenomenon which in these poems exceeds that which is simply temporally past. The nostalgia performed here is poetic but never sentimental. The *then*, rather, appears almost as a separate entity: something wounded but which is nursed and kept alive; something to which intimate sacrifices have been made to appease and pacify it; something forgiven and yet which still despairs of the possibility of forgiveness. Memory of the *then* stakes a brutal ethical claim on the *now*. But it is the grief of love, not malice, which keeps the wounds of the *then* tender and open. The epigraph from Rilke about the newly present absence of a departed friend hovers like one of his dark angels entirely over the *disputatio* style of the *Summa Solemnis*, which is marked throughout by loss and all its painful iterations and recapitulations, "in the crestfallen gestures that mothers make/When the womb cannot take," or in those increasingly futile efforts in the wake of a grief to recall precisely the distinctive scent or laugh of the lost one for whom we grieve.

It is thus neither accidental nor incidental that one poem references Rome's Janiculum hill, the antique site of the cult of Janus, that two-faced god of time, transitions, passageways, beginnings, endings, doorways, archways, and gates, who is simultaneously looking backwards and looking forwards. The poems channel Janus to witness to the all-too-human experience of duality: both fragility and permanence, contingency and necessity, decomposition and re-composition, unmaking and re-making, past and future, spirit and flesh are affirmed, though the balance ultimately tilts in the closing lines of *Summa Solemnis* toward the finality of the God who "*alone can cross the infinite endings/And bring thyself from the threshold of home into home.*" Everywhere in this poetic *memento mori* the shadows of death, loss, and grief creep in and chasten—but do not and cannot extinguish outright—the hope the poet professes, even if in the darkest vales and valleys that difficult act of hope seems to be more of the order of T.S. Eliot's in "Ash Wednesday," a hope which seems (if not is) indistinguishable from its renunciation.

In these poems, Smith Gilson does not shy away from acknowledging and even celebrating the fragility, the failures, and the "littleness" of the brief, liminal expanse of any given human life hanging tenuously between two perfections. Her oblique allusions to the *ubi sunt* motif of medieval poetry, an entire genre given over to the damning question of "Where are they now?" (represented best, perhaps, by François Villon's "Ballade des dames du temps jadis," which asks, *Mais où sont les neiges d'antan?* ["Where are the snows of yesteryear"?]) keep the verities of human transience to the fore. Furthermore, the poems also roundly embrace the theme of "littleness," here perhaps with what might be nods both to the Little Way of St. Thérèse of Lisieux as well as Julian of Norwich's arresting vision of all that has been created telescoped to the size of a little hazelnut enclosed in the palm of God's hand. "I will stay," the speaker says in "Mater Dolorosa Memento Mei," educing the image of a well-worn rosary, "in another decade of my own or another life/Sewn into the cross stitches in the littleness we own." Elsewhere in the poems "littleness" appears in the little way of holy domesticities of sewing, cooking, caring for children, in the gift and the task of all the many private graces and exertions of family life in common. *Mater* and matter are together byways to the divine.

It may well be that Smith Gilson has Charles Péguy's holy but ordinary repetitions in mind here and throughout the volume, such that the repetitions of seemingly routine and mundane acts throughout a person's earthly life cohere or are translated into a bridge, laid end to end, which brings her into heaven. Whether or not Péguy is a proximate source, both the performance and the theme of repetition provide an interpretive clue about how best to read and inhabit this set of poems. In terms of performance, repetitions of lines and images occur not only within a singular poem but are recursive *between* them as well; the borders between the poems and even the two ostensibly separate cycles are thus porous, leaky, permeable. These literary repetitions provide continuity and coherence to the collection in much the same way as there is continuity of the self from birth to death to eschatological transfiguration, from our "sweating Selves; but worse" (Hopkins) to that moment, "in the twinkling of an eye, at the last trump . . . [where] we shall be changed" (1 Corinthians 15:52).

And in terms of content, repetition gets raised to the order of the thematic. One line from "Farewell Sestina" in particular recalls Péguy, in which the poet writes that "I am the repeated drama of the little things." But more than this, perhaps, is the sense that the kind of repetition that builds and rebuilds the self is the repetition found in the liturgy. The poems are entirely suffused with liturgical, especially penitential rhythms, from the "ashes to ashes/dust to dust" of Ash Wednesday which inaugurates the season of Lent (there are references to "coarse Lenten cloth," "late Lenten tears," "Lenten gray," "Lenten hope," "Lenten rain," the "Lenten lily," among others) to the awaited joys of Eastertide. The poems reveal and revel in the sacramental repetitions of the Eucharistic formulae ("Blessed are those who are called to the supper of the Lamb;" "Only mouthe the words and I shall be healed;" "I am not worthy to enter under your roof") and receptions of the Eucharistic host, whenever "Sunday has come again" or, finally, as food for the (final) journey, where the "viaticum dissolves/When swallowed/ Unnoticed as it moves/How repetition soothes . . . " ("Ad Secundum: Mortalitas et Caritas").

These poems are a true gift, especially for the Catholic reader. In certain respects, they are in the register of prayer, a space where the deepest desires of the human heart call out to the deepest desires of the divine heart, where "deep calls out to deep" (*abyssus abyssum invocate*, Psalm 42:7). The speaker of the poems surely recalls the ambivalences of the biblical psalmist, by turns grateful, raw, bitter, erotic, laudatory, elegiac, imprecatory, choleric, sad. The beauty and the honesty of Smith Gilson's collection of poems invites readers into the luminous heart of an anguished, broken world where Christ nevertheless is near and where nothing is ever truly lost.

Jennifer Newsome Martin
THE UNIVERSITY OF NOTRE DAME

TREGENNA HILL

OFFICE OF THE DEAD

It all began with a bare lime tree
Where neither fairness nor faint citrus arose again
Years have passed as no man numbers

Deep calls to deep in the voice of your waterfalls

Speak a slow tongue to me
Let your words transpire from body to bead and back again
Let the floodgates breathe
Heaven's Lenten hope has gone too far

A confession falls along the sidelined shade of faith
Tangled and tossed among sounds
Your causes and effects have a scent and a trail
My insides pulse with the form of your perfume

Poor souls are we
Never ending never crossing the divide
Suspects in a kiss
Your God will not abide
Let His angels fall asleep
Then kiss my sides
In you I have winters to confuse

All your whirlpools and waves have passed over me

Forgiveness restores love through the very love it lacks
The littleness of their faces
Round down the sharpened corners
And stacked edges of our in-between
Ave Maria etched in sea and sun
Amid beauty to recollect
And freedom to forget

I never was very good for you
Even my confessions come and go
An overgrown arcadia's glow
Wrestling the thicket of nonbeing
You are the slowness
 You are the virtue among these scenes

You are dying the gentle death daily
With a day shaped silhouette
Formed of penance and sunset
Folded and loaded tears
Sear as citrus cuts
So much cover upon cover
Trespass and remind

Only the irreducible endures and resurrects
She who forgives is in debt
A debtor
Using what she lacks in order to receive what she lacks
And then with nothing more than a half-turned glance
Glimpses her resurrected body

My love
Every word is excessive
A rose of scented failures
Covering the lover of daily forms
Folded and gentle
Ripping forth a brief burst
The golden pulp strips itself from the cream
And a mandarin sun in your mouth bruises mine

In your backyard
The hills howl the agony of a dying sun
Purple crocuses calm and then thrust
Heaves of color washed with late Lenten rain
Ground the lore between pauses

Mocked innocence resurrects resistance

For the passive moment pressed ahead
Stains the lilies crushed and cajoled
Accursed and cut off for the sake of you

Once when there was time
And I was still I
The hills mounted with color and cursed
Cursed us with their ecstatic blooms
Cursed us with their perfection
Cursed us with their kind of time

Soft and eternal in a bloom
On hair
On face
In hands
Wistful fingers twirling goodbye
Till again
Till again
Till we meet again my hesitant failing
Sacraments chained us to such happiness
And became our fear

Life of love
Love among the ruins
The gentle and the gentlest

I am neither gentle nor dying
But the runoff of sworn words
Excess honey and water
Demanding the crisp white veil

Heal me in the voice of thy floodgates
You are the shake and the standstill
You disturb the depths that call upon depths
In desperate neglect and rogue innocence
Come now
What a riot of sadness of unflinching sight

Of wildflowers at your gate

The fallen waterfalls fall over me in fallow form
After the first things
After the contraries
After the response
I am not I
I am still not I
When will the depths call forth the depths in the voice of thy floodgates?
When will you speak a slow tongue to me?

The green is shattered by the snows of last winter
A testament thrown back against the wall
One sound comes to a thud and falls safely away
Insistent young veils huddle around the corridor
Tiny ants making haste in the wind
Breaching the apple core
Rotted and soft
A cathedral bell throbs into the dark and cool

Throngs of hope enter the gate
Now is the time for my love to come thaw his lack
Chase me and chasten this static beauty
I was neither fit for tears nor the forgiveness that nears

A holy order a holy rosary
The hot smell of the coal and the cool switch of perfumes
Transfuses my shade into a soul
The scent of clean soap clung against the distance
And transposed the empty chalice
Ivy covered words climb and call forth among themselves
Gestures haunt in the afterglow of long lined faces
Their crosses cut paths and hunt me down
Tangled amid sounds
Nothing more
No nothing more
Could shore up this doubt
And undo all the years

AGNUS DEI MEMENTO MEI

Warm bread pulled apart from the hidden seam
And roads full of dotting trees
Young and old
Little branches twirling in chaotic perfection
Around and around we fall back in a swing of memory

You come into the cool and rare
Once common and warm
And there was the present
Present for the little lambs of God
Who remember me then

What was then lives among the eternal juniper and rhyming June
When snowless seasons spend too fast the lilac tread
The smells and sounds abound and round off bright then gray
At the tips of fingers ten

Counting on countless time in the abundance of laughter
Scattered papers and fresh dairy
Candles and white cakes
A world of sacred mantles

Up ahead we dip into the next scene
Little farms in the latter edges
Limes and lemon trees
Intoxicant fields and warmth endless warmth

The sun erected and bright goes along
In us and through us
You must have said some perfection
So far along in words

In the unspeakable and glorious difference
You mouthed my words
And reclaimed the eternal line

Blessed are those who are called to the supper of the Lamb

We are once and for all passengers of past perfections
We do and have always done what is ahead
Behind us there was something
Some one thing that I am
One separated and dead perfection
You were the laughter
Laughter in this room

In the common and warm
The sun answers with a brighter hue
Flashes hit the hills
And mount new scenery to scourge our silence

Up and around the gate
Forsake the second hand in the late sun
In the leisure of the lost and found
Bursting into a phantasm of drinks and smokes
Bursting beyond the flesh
The bells and wines mellow
Architectural epiphanies
Cypress trees
Yellow sunsets that blind and float

These days are an elusive substance of grace
Held with late light
Smoke burns the back of throats
Completing its threat around your face
A high moon you said
In a hesitant failing your beauty welled again
The gods and angels found themselves satisfied
And we sang again
Satisfy the sanctity of a moment

Point and swell with beauty and sing again
Backs among grasses
Rasped voices muddled in the undertow
Sprawling features pantomiming wildly on a balcony
A ledge where gods would be happy
You leap into the cool and rare
Calm warm and common then

We scatter back to the cobble's rabble
Checkered wet streets sink in
We mount and ruin and fail in our plans
Chatter renews confidence
A newness imbued on your face and hands

Everything is forgotten but hot smells and sweat
The oven glove against my face
You take fast and take my clothes
Summer sinks in to one long drink
In the in-between status between shade and form
I am the warmth of some substance of grace

In the eternal moment that escapes what might have been
God wouldn't mind if I overtook Him
For one round of the hand
For I am now and only now
Your slow shift from shade to flesh
You slip your life in mine
Forgive me
My lover of daily forms
For I was never more than a moment in your time

Thick sand obliterated all other thoughts
Sand from the revolt of the gods
Lacryma Christi trembling in singeing joy
Stores of my *ubi sunt* coiling down
To the place of the furies where
Broken perfections no longer forgive

Where are those who were before us?

The moth's ecstatic curse
Finds candles at the Cross
Precariously dangled firsts things offer their remorse

Pressing and receding into the night
I am I for the *then* and the now
I am I for the cool and the rare

Then has passed and with it your nearness
And it is all yours to claim
You are now so uncommon
A warm recollection presses and recedes from sight
Never a slow tongue
Never fade from my sight

Never forgive me for the death of sweet suffering things
For flooded fruits ready to give over
The depths of the floodgates have passed over me and go by way of your
    nearness

MATER DOLOROSA MEMENTO MEI

I will stay in another decade
Where lilacs push past their scent and serenade
Where forms always fail and fall into the other
What a beautiful and intolerable ruin you were!

Earthworms writhe in the heat and hide
Clayware stained and dried with sand
The passages of strawberries hitting soil
Moisture comes and goes along these walls
Yellow and bright stucco smoothed by our hands
Such a hideous yellow
A glorious color for laughter under cover

I will stay in another decade of my own or another life
Sewn into the cross stitches in the littleness we own
Another life can sink its teeth into the olives
And find no more resistance than the stone
Rolled around in the mouth and on the tongue
Ten years seem nothing more than a farmstand
And a standing sun

Ten years can neither claim envy nor resolve
So small you are
You sink your teeth into my arms
I will stay in another way in the desolate church yard
Hail Mary full of grace
Your face of sorrows stands timeless and patterned

Ten fewer words will be said
I am not worthy to enter under your roof again
The blasphemer's resolve
Silent and signing
Ten years can claim neither substance nor change the depth
Where I am again and again calling forth from your gates

Domine memento mei cum veneris in regnum tuum

Say neither words nor peace
Only stare your incomparable stare
Your face
Your palms that can erase
Put your hands on my head and on my face
Place the distance between the years
Hear me Mary
Mother of sorrows and trespassed wits
Hear my awful prayer

Let your Lamb of God bear these brutish fears
And the brunt of all my cares

Remember me when you come into your kingdom

In another decade
In another town
The sound of red potatoes thud the tin and soften
The quickened wafting passage from field to mouth
In heat and water
The sound of young birds
Flood my little flutter

You have eviscerated every holed up wall
Where memory should neglect
Here is my consent for death
The words are clear
A clearing upon the fields
In the office of the dead hear my prayers
Neither eternity nor spirit could obscure my cares
Only for the body and for its duration
Only for the love felt so much like fear

We volley for the roughest lips in a violet maze
I climb the tree and throw down the seeded fruit
You handle the apple wrapped in rote leather

And suffocate it to its root

I am in your body and in your duration
I share in its slow salted appeal

Your thoughtful decomposition steals and salivates
And grasps the nearness of my Lenten lily

Resumed with every consolation of regret
I am one damnation spent resisting a decade in time
Hair thin and spread between
I am neither spirit nor flesh
But one figure watching the silkscreen

Among the rafters' heaving planks
Among a shade breathing color and lines
Considerations of past beauty chastise these eyes
Your blank collection flows tiredly behind

How beautiful is a day without claim
Without eternal lore
Considerations of past beauty reconsider their time
What a lovely sunset to even the score

An unfinished aesthete cleans his late winter skates
One dinner between us
One decade to go
Slow ink and unction
And ice condemn your form
I dare against its sacrament with one minute more

In a minute more
In a nature with jabs to its core
The fish find their lines timed in cool streams
Swallowing these sighs of mine

A glorious gray shore
A dot in the distance

You bow for measure
My winter wish is wrestled to the still
Framed you are by the stained wooden sill

A face in the fading fight
A slip of a shade
Bring back the stick and glue of new pine comb
Traded between two hands

I am, it is and all things are:

Recollected aftermaths long after the fact

A foreign wartime song
Enchants the steep embankment
Claiming one immeasurably subtle sand of sleep

I am, it is and all things are:

Brittle on an edge and tinkering with a tan

An unendurable inclusion ran over my face
The gentle migratory nature of your hands
Was replaced by the first and last place
An address
A city block
Anonymous bustle and buses

You brush my hair
Artifacts of neglected wishes
Trace the past beauty idolatrously intact

Signs of little known age find Spring in the snow
My confessor was near and never so alone
He'll never find that night of yours so gentle and calm
This artificial language came with its prattle and balm
Pathos of past presentiments have rounded the bend
Childlike in a long December's end

SONG FOR THE FLESH

In a moment consumed and crushed
We all believe what is blessed

You confuse me in this short lot
In you I feel what is too good to be true
You bewilder eternity with a body
With a heavenly body
With a body and a face with kisses graced

I believe I can kiss the very presence of prior kisses
Permeating the present with your presence

You are the wheeler's clay
The solemnity between cycles
The warm May
The underlying unformed day
The quiet at a Passion play
You are the rhyme and sway

Your blood is on the whip wince and call
You load the deck with the breath of a dying God
You are the shorelines of the cay
White foam into clear blue
Wave upon wave
Fold upon fold
Flesh upon flesh
Unrepentantly precious and small
You disappear after the third fall

You are the perfected final fall gracing me with your knees
A good day kept at bay with every blade of grass
Distinct and intact
You are the indivisible between facts
You are the sayings at drawn shades

You are the surreal in all surrender
A performance in every bloodstain
From dusk to dawn
You are the nonchalant and tender nod

Husk the corn
Keep the time
Place worn hands on hair
A brilliant sheen in every cloak
You share the secret promise to return
Your words lay like clover as I learn

I am softening for you in this pain
I am sanctifying every whim and bone
You are the keeper's collection solving my perpetuation

The selected and descanted force
The sweet nothing bracing my thighs with fragrant force
You are the perfume of the perfume
You are the black night where music blooms
A confused frankincense weeping honeysuckle
You are every infinitely suffering thing

A pantheist's dream

You are the steam on shocked ice
I feel the grooves of little dents and roll the dice
Inside
Outside
You are the diving curve of my bitten lip
Pine cone and lemon peel and reams of nature's whip

I am the youngest skin in a sweat salt body stealing all difference
I am the season of anticipation
You are the reason blindfolding reason

I am I for the then that claims me now
An Atlantic night cold and tight

One dull towel
Little fur- and little light
Water forgive me
Night of all nights forgive me

In primrose and cotton
I feel your parched lips waxed smooth
Your heavy fabrics chaff and clutch
For touch I forsake you
My God I have forsaken you

Again and again I will do so
So forgive me by denying me your forgiveness
For flesh and blood can go too far

Forgive me with a finite hand
End this infinite and eternal lust
Hush me mightily
For flesh and blood have gone too far

I ask of you what I ask of neither man nor angel:
I ask you to forgive me by denying me your forgiveness

Give me the grave as grave
Give me a finite grace
Give me the soil as soil
Give me what finitudes erase
Give me the tyrant's kiss
For I am the other as other ever sold and without a hold

Save me with my own betrayal
Save me with the quiet well of a forgiven but forgotten fate

In the haste of the Janiculum hill
Salvati
Salvami
In the hanging soft dust
Salvati

Salvami
In the grace of your already given time
Salvati
Salvami

Abyssus abyssum invocat in voce cataractarum tuarum; omnes gurgites tui
  et fluctus tui super me transierunt

In the voice of thy floodgates
I ask of you what I ask of neither man nor angel:
Give me the royal road of the Holy Cross and let yourself forget

Forget your testament and my time
Forget your eternal givenness
Your lips locked on mine
I was never the other as other
I deny my fingers the real shape of your sign
Make me forget the scented pines

The warmth of the bread pulled apart forgive me
The balcony and its swarming bees forgive me
Salvati
Salvami

Forget the honey extended in warmth
Forgive the sweet tar stinging my lips
Flesh and blood can go too far

So far in forgiveness
Let me forget the perfect pull inside me
And the taste of its brine forging a taste I can no longer sign
Let me forget these sweet suffering things
With one ounce of your time

The separated body never stops to make the sign
Engines are dying down and paying the heavy fine
Every pull tops the other and laughs in resolute accord
From our Lady to our Lord

Salvati
Salvami

Deny me the cool brink between earth and lake
Forget the calculated risks
Remake me with the emptiness of your love
Forgive me in your repeated perfection

The freezing water has forgiven me
Its brutality forgives me
Salvati
Salvami

Forget me so that I can no longer revolt
Against my abstractions and your Grace

We have let this creature go too far
So I ask of you what I ask of neither man nor angel
Take me home
To the homeless home
Take me to the ground's own logic and race
Trace the lost tracings

My reckless sorrow neither outwits nor abides
Some terrible hope has asked for a master
I am at your side
What a lovely little story tried and hanged
The blessings of two legs rearranged

Let the waterfalls fall over me
My neediness consumes me
Needful hope hopes for a lovely little story
One story
For little loves crawling across stretched sycamore and its silent stage

THE SONG OF THE SPIRIT

You come near
Too near for me to feel your bare body disappear
And I think you are still here
Hearing my cares

Heavy and light
With the succor of summering things
We trim the night

God nor angels could crave to spare
What you spare
You spare me the pause between descriptions
Before hills surmount with green
Before lilacs embrace the box
Before the pine fresh cuts trace the sodden lots
And cloister sensation

On inverted perfections and verdant patches
Plovers lay their spotted eggs
And we wrestle with our demonic age

The smell of the pale lilac lover's thrust
Redeems me and bursts in us
You are with me now
You are drifting into a circle of rhymes

Come home wearing the lost and found
Roundabout wave upon wave
Save the day
Save me one wink of eternity
One spot on the gilded caravan

The hermit shells scurry over
The low tide Cornwall sand

Every discovery and every lover
Every exposed land
Every little nest to pour our frames
Every weed
Every rummage
Every ocean
Every bow and kiss
Ends as it begins

The song of the spirit fails us
Inertia of ended hopes
Gives ground to your swirling words
Your lips to cheek and tongue
I taste what can be undone

In the thoughtless Spring
Meditations of joy rocked our feet and faded
Funny how you left your socks on
As the day traded for the cool coax of night

Funny how small spaces that could save us
Are trapped in the collection net
Its string thickens into cord and chokes me
And I am I in the fate
With gills still pumping lashing and writhing

The song of the spirit
The dying breath
In and through every contrary
You have fated it all

When the way up
Claims the rented hopes of the way down
You have fated it all

Your touch hot and dry
Your kiss solitary and on the cheek
From the rosy to the pale

You have fated it all

A shared glass links lips in mutual sound
In the contrary
In the rented
In the solitary and in the pale
You have fated it all

See the ice melt and the lips retract
The cheeks find their wetness and touch finds its gloves

It is freezing now
In a winter near a lake
On a decade to forsake
One decade with sweetness
With cheeks bordering on lips
Bordering the black sand
Borders of massive sensation resisting all resurrection

You are the prelude to Good Friday
The loads and the limits
Like unto like
A glacial refrain wiping two fingers across lip stains
Your orders persist through the midnight consecration
You are the Lenten hope having gone too far

Funny how little things violate my demand
For an empty little land
A little dream cottage you said with every dream gone
Its closed shutters shuttering down
Shut down dust dismantling the clean floor

Pollens and dusts and old lusts
Found on jackets set aside
Hard coverings and pictures
Describe their glorious asides

Rhyming words with less reason

Was our reason for loving them to their ends
To the ends of the earth that span across your face

We whiled the weeks away in your hand
Forgot the future and its empty stand
Forgiven by the then that conquers me now
The ambiguity hints at the rare
To the rare so cursed in its perfection
And common then

Senseless beauty
Senses for beauty
Beautiful senses
And the sense of beauty
We never minded the first shove
And off to bed sleepy head

I hear the song of the spirit
The gate closes
The wind has its icy sink
I dip my head in its heaviness
The clinking porch bells
Heavy as lead into the wayside
Mourn and meander for miles as I go

My goodnight night
Your sighs of love
Little lights unlit
Drawn baths un-breached
Hit me wind
Hit me water
Hit me with your forsaken space
Hit me wine
I need your apathetic grace to quiet me now

Singing collects the cap
The backbone of lonely abstraction spills over
I stop to crave what it spares

Careless in the plural figures of your perfect walk

The lines underneath your lips
Smooth into a smile
Knees have their ghost's infection
Weakened with less than substance
More than breath
Between the nude and pale
A threefold winding cloth set aside
We scale the night of loaned lies

I ask you what I ask of neither God
Nor His devils
Nor His angels
Nor His time and its pair eternity
Nor His nearness and its fair pasture
Nor His visitation and its *contra mundum*
Nor any other of His creatures that can fast and fall

I ask you not to recount the passing decade staking out the loss
An unkind hope haunts the last break
The fruit lays open and the painter is neither appalled nor sorrowful
As I am now

GOZO TO PATMOS

How our little loves loved my crepes
And called them so many other names
In a thicket of clotted sugar and butterflies
Faces dissolve the momentary fright
And heighten our monumental fear

None stay long enough
To blush past the winter's rose
Ashes to ashes
Dust to dust

Old words and new thoughts
Seizing their little molds at three and five
Before numbers are counted
Before the numbness sets in
Breathe them in

The seaside pail
The early mail
The frantic call
Shivers embraced
Warm and racing rosebuds under the palm trees

They undress the scenery at every corner
Simple and majestic
Two hawthorns sharp and red
White and pink flowers
Around them
A cameo profile of faces chameleon and mute
A deck on a harbor
Sails opened and closed
In and out
In the old and new

Their golden hair flickers in the sunbeams as they lay
We are thoughtless words
Alifeless accord
Folded still for their stay
For the light water brush and wanderlust play
We should be wordless thoughts

Ancient scenes reign over our pith and death
Acted out in soldiered form
Tears are thick and shorn with fright
We are faceless cutouts from endless heights

Write your names in the English sand
                        and watch the waves come in
Trace the bastion
                        and watch the waves come in
Draw the curling petals
                        and watch the waves come in

Hushing me helplessly
I breathe the blooming lilies and mums on the box
The bees find their way all fat and stung
Go on window sill
Go on
Bring me to life to life
To the joy spent in furious hope
Holding on and hinting at your love

Hit me roses
Hit me wine
Hit me with the smell of a warm kitchen
Wrapped in the cadence of endlessly forgiving chimes

The mellow rake passes over
Summer to winter
Mythic Sunday lines
Nothing more and nothing less
Than little birds with open mouths and bent knees

Bruised with the sap and switch of solemnity's tree

You alone crack open the form
And can comprehend
The lapsing moment where I am now
A passenger of past perfections

Outside
A bare lime tree with withered skins
Inside
Clay tiles recollecting under foot
Through the window
A lake neglectful of its historic order
Toddling in the dwindling sun

Outside
Inside
Through the window
Past noon
Past the sacramental table
Mother Mary understand
Your child must be the branches floor and sand

You are the sentimentalist's anarchy
Never cautious with grief upon grief
Come see the thumbprints and the oils
That stand-in over the lapse of time

The glory of this meaningless love
Past nature
Past condition
The split down a back
Closing and heavy eyes
Breath with separated lips
I watch for a moment
The wanton moment wins with shy relief
And universal lies

I deny the divisible with the divisible
And fan the centurions of despair
You are nothing more than flesh and blood
One heart relentlessly swallowed by its own beat
You are the lent and imported wisdom
The stand-in that stands alone

Beyond the need for grace
Fallen leaves become a thing of grace
They are the remains that remain intact after the fact
Tarrying along in every word
Be the faith after the aftermath
Be the hope after the aftermath
Be the love after the aftermath
Only mouthe the words
Only mouthe the words and I shall be healed

A wet fog rolls in and with it the kind clarity of ended motives
One remote star bails us out of deep trodden night
And fills me in with the form I am
I am the pretended good
So beautiful and good to quicken these senses

Harbor of tears
The last imprint of Christ
A swift tender and mournful cry
As the spear lances His side
The form of futility
The Good that does not end
The perfume of pure pattern
Breaking the distance
And for no good reason but love
He is the honey and the water
The sweetness in every thirst
The descent of every dove

The distance and the divide
The lost life among orchard trees

Swift to bloom and fall
We are
Insisted charms
Indefatigable harm
We are nothing more than empty arms

In this thy hour one blade of grass resists
And I pull and pull for the wine in the water

The monk has his cowl
The nun her veil
The church has its bells
All of them field our covetous tears

The highway of shelled out and darting vacancies
Passes with silver and alms
The royal road will appease us as it promised
Promising little girls

Mother Mary understand
My life is on your lips
Your child must be the branches floor and sand

OUR HAPPINESS HAS UNMADE US

Our happiness has unmade us
waiting with mythic grace
Taste the fresh milk
Crack the bright egg in all its whiteness
Cut through with some unbearable yellow
Hit with the fragrance of June

Into the bowl and into the pan
Mixed up with exotic fruit
From little hands with ideas of other lands

The cotton is white upon white
And I can see through to you
How your laughter soothes
Laughing on the other side!

My Love holds his hope in a tree
In fifty Eastertides
Faithful and pastel kisses
Do try to make room for me

I find no other happiness than this June
Of all the Junes in a decade

I am these days and no more
Than the softness of petals poured
With petulance and resistance and youth

I am the happy body sunk back into the wooden booth
Baskets checkered with cloth
Russet colors under lighter reds
Where pairings are dwindled down in the hot dusk
To one
Wine and stilton

Or two
Hand in hand in the English countryside

Hail to the Cotswalds
Hail to the names of their arcadian towns
So many syllables who could frown
We are upside down and it was never so right
Our pictures are taken in the *then*
As now never was

Your Eliot read on a Wednesday bed
Intertwined footpaths in a Coker fog
Hail to the sign pointing right
To the driver on the left
Troubadours confused and exalted
Happily led
Kindness and kin and fear
Following your forethoughts in the *then*

The rain
The rain
The rain makes the day
A plotting hill
One slow scene
The sacrificial pain of God
Weeping agencies of beauty beyond beauty
Silent stones and grey wool
Half words and dates
The chill on your cheeks

Saturday waits
The vicarage waits
Resurrected dust
One corner of the Fall
A prefect of the Fall

Be brave in dusk's Holy hour
This inebriate and inviolate wisdom

Finds the keenest blade and sanctifies the sloping ridge

In our thoughts
In our words
In the hollow of the turn-sister's slated wall
In the beginning and in the end
Mother Mary my life is on your lips

The cautious organ plays
Papers arranged
Perfect rain
Rain
Perfect and momentary rain

You are the highest poverty
The verity of nothing
You lift the veil of my foreign sorrow

The dead have their endless wait
Forged in the blood we drank
God of silence
God of love
Lover of our silence
Silencing our loves
You are on the other side of the cloth
In the longer lines I crawl
Unmade in every myth
My life is on your lips
Only mouthe the words
Only mouthe the words and I shall be healed

YOUR ENDURING INELEGANCE

In the country of the quiet man
Your enduring inelegance
Has pared me down
Strained clouds pierced with light
Forgiven by an ashen day

Insurmountable scenery flooded the cleft
From the hills to the shine on your chin
To the left lean bone china and straw sunsets
Break like bread with heat and life

Warm and worn down couches
Creaked with country sounds
Encroaching faint hours and throated doves
Crept in time intrinsic to your beating chest
Graceful and graceless love
Arrested in an eternally temporal consecration

In the city
Blotted passions and convected tears
Sonatas play
Aeschylus lays low in the nearing spires
Tragic beers slung cold
The same chants and cheers
Chain your glow

In the beginning and in the end
Save the gods old and new
One act can save us if it be holy

In country
In city
In beginning and end
You bring curvature to my cheek

As I wait

In the fall smoke
In the tall pines
I am hit with the curve around the bend
In the fog of the drink
In the fog of the streets

Come with me and wait without hope

Mary of Magdala
It's *maudlin* my love
The college name
Surreptitious and never the same
Roll the stone away
Roll it away
Towards the winding lane

The dotted ports with cohorts and gypsies
Our imported wine leapt back
To the Italian countryside
Burns with its cheers
No matter how mellow or kind

Here is Shropshire
With verdant lines
You say green
You laugh at my language
I mouthe your words

Roll the stone away
Roll it away
Towards the winding lane
Mary and her lost paradise
A precious bane bails out your perfection
Stand near to me
Read to me
Hear me

As I mouthe your meaning

Read to me with divine lamentation
For dearly I love you
In such a green land!

Twenty-something rounds the decade with an extra year
Shrewsbury in the clearing trees
Dark deer desolate forgiveness and a failed tongue
Come to me
Wash over my eyes
and invent the threat of the nearing hour

Roll the stone away
Roll it away
Towards the winding lane
Peek in the low door
Remind me of Assisi
Lips and hands pressed to the floor

In the stand in over nothingness
As subtle as dead perfume
You are the bravery beneath lost causes
The sacramental plaint of primal sorrow

You are the burnt out cathedral of a God forsaken town
Cut down with eternity in your precious Coventry
I wait without sensation

The sacred hills are scarred with Spring
In the unmade future remade brick by brick
I wait without sensation
Your rough and coarsely shaven face
Your hushed and hesitant failing
Never new thoughts
Never new being
Be still
Tuck me in with the elegance of Kierkegaard

A grief observed
A descent of the dove
A love as fear

The fall
The fall
The fall folds into me
Into that future place of past redemption

Brown roots raise a collateral cause
Slow sap weakens the branches
I imagine we collide
with soil on our sides

In this mile
Ocean
Field
In all my open treasons
In your enduring inelegance you have pared me down
Chesterton's house
A Beaconsfield lunch rushed to the rambles of rage
Children children
Resembling our kind in the hours past
When last things are the only things that last

Snowfalls born of sentiment
Shoring up the hills with anguished ecstasy
In this thy hour
One resignedly small
Bat squeak of hope
Chaffs the spot where cures became man

In the place of the furies
Swift comes the lightning
Striking the dark road
For a moment I can see your tears and your reddened nose
And the frail hint of my life on your lips

You deny it all
You deny me your kiss
And I ask of you what I ask of neither God nor his angels
Let something unfit for words run through my hips
Euclidian logic never fails
But I ask for its failure
A trail of miserable finalities
Braves these racing remains
Down for the count and counting on eternity
We are sailors knots turned inside out
Long souls stretched along
Cocktail ghosts
Acquaintances that make laughter with little sayings
Laughter is the spell that breaks the boughs and lets us fall

I fall for every artifact unkind or kind
Late night alchemy rails against partition
Combining our contrition

Pare me down
Cut me down
Cover me with the cloth
Take away my sins

Roll the stone away
Roll it away
Towards the winding lane

The fragrant silk and rind
A late harvest rot root
A perfect night wine
An immovable moment
Young life blinks and whines

Closed expressions and coverlids
The Paschal sun and seeping mint tea
The snail's tiny and constant shadow
In every hill and ledge

In every artifice of monastic wish
The edge of your kiss
Ends as it begins

Poor souls never cross the divide
They crucify what coincides
In a hundred Eastertides
In the burst before the June tide
In the backdrop of a delinquent moon
Your enduring inelegance has pared me down

Lips press and press
The church has its bells
The peddler a little hymn to sell
Sold I am by its sound

Hands hold the shape of little cups
Eyes split the infinity between the lusted and the lost
You are the intolerable ruin leaning over the altar
The reflected face on gloss
You are the worm that rounds the wood

A bent head asks for forgiveness
Forgiven by sacrifice
Your God lowers the axe like a veil
Your God becomes my God

Senseless tales
Scented wax and remorse
The never more
Forgive me in a fourfold score
I am not I
Nor never was my word
Neither was I the sunlit lace
Nor the light along a resigning soft face
I have no knowledge of any kind
That would forgive me this time

I never was the kind of creature
Kind enough to redeem these chronological schemes
Bringing back a pulse requires eternity you see
When the forest and the thicket murmur
When the doves lunge
And the bells swell with gold
Swell with me against the hunter and his tide

When this plunging cool plum bails out my throat
From speaking reasonless words
When I taste the sweetness
That only the union of a soul and flesh procure
Then can I flood your memory in a standstill?

Lost life divides the last of the closing snow
My life is a defeated demonstration
of weakened knees and velvet bees
Hell's enduring abstractions seize me
Thawed in the last recorded touch
Under dawn and dusk

Sub specie aeternitatis
Dark deer
The glint of eyes
Sliced fruit on the wood rail
Seeds scattering halos
Overgrown grass
A stone Madonna
A grey hammock left untouched
Everything that is given
Is given with secondary formation

The wild beast is caught
It fights to flee and falls on my knees
I am
It is
All things are
Hardly there or near

And with hearts still pumping

In a forest of fallen senses
Favoring the worsening season
I hold till something buckles black in my eyes
And gives way

I am the passing moth's moment
With thinned wings before the flame
Cracking till nothing
The thick crash
Dissolving into light ash
I am
It is
All things are
Down for the count and counting on a gentle death

IN THE COWER

Blotted and sullen shadows sit on the curtains
And play chess with the hours

They show us the holy privilege
A coda of the Passion

The trees grow a kind of grist against the sediment
Their lonely teeth cut into the soft and wild passage

They show us the holy privilege
A coda of the Passion

Lashes pilot your eyes
Closed for a moment
And the late world falls apart in the rain
You are the supplicant
The basement
The shelter that remains after the fact

We fall aligned into a ready-made shade
We own so little of this nothingness
This shivering frightful stone

Put your hand on every orifice
Close in on some substance of heart
Press into me
Bring me back to form
In the urge before the cower
Never ready to give over

Every insufficient means
A coda of the Passion

You are the gentle dying
A coveted wilted robe
You outdo my ragged little body
And its shared halfwit agonies

You are the far-fetched sacrifice
The bravery between scenes
Hollow me out and fill me in

Every insufficient means
A coda of the Passion

I want neither to survive the heavy heel in the mud
Nor its tread breathing like an asp between each step

I will do you no harm
I am solely a spirit without a soul
Only a half soul or a shade
A memory of the undertow
Stuffed down my throat
I sing a muted call

My dear
Let me endure your confusions
You are my confusion

But how can I endure the gentleness of a gentle death?
Your taste on my flesh bites back
and riles in the passing age

Do not laugh in the form I have not passed
The dancing cold hand warns with burning thighs
And I have begun to feel old
In the littleness I own

Every confusion you said
Every confusion we began and never ended
Is a coda of the Passion

You are the easiness imbued around a face
An ancient restoration resolved
My sights drill your graceless remains
In the stand-in over nothingness
Break me with your life
For once in your life break me with your life

Solemnity's pillow is buried deep in the snow
The iceman cometh with phantom wants and woe
Shattered ice and the wisp of your cigarette
Shattered ice and the sting of your face

Every confession you said
Every confession we began and never ended
Is a coda of the Passion

The olive intoxicated in its preservation
jolts me to its hidden time
In the eternal decomposition of your soul and mine
Make the sign of the Cross
Once more or never more
Favor the fable
And follow the flesh

Passengers of past perfections
Lay beside the holy privilege
The honeybee and the clover and its wanderlust arcadia
Become a coda of the Passion

THE SONG OF THE SOUL

Neglected innocent whims
Snow cherries and slim lips
These are nothing but wreckages of my shape

I will tackle this sweetness until its pit
A writ against nature and bordering brown
Stops me momentarily
From crushing you thoroughly through the eiderdown
Long after you tire

I am the locked soul in a high Mass
I hear the caroler's plough whistling to the field
Cutting freely and without hesitation
Wistful and without regard
Nature laying down her cards

The floods winnow
The wasps whine incessantly
Rid of their hidden nest
We rake the spruce with agnate pattern
Spread I am
A winter's veil removing your sighs

In a lulling contest
Lakes of sweat chide your thighs
Dry and needful mouths
We drink water from one glass

Ice censures the silence
The most solicitous of guests has arrived:
It is your laughter
Laughter in this room

Laughter after exhaustion spills into the kitchen

The dusk of dinner
Fuss and pans
Getaway plans

Summer threatens the autumn law
Consubstantiating our hope in its run
In this room
Your laughter sinks the sun

Tomatoes
Camparis bunched
Smell of that hot sun
Bleeding instant gifts

We are
Shifting through papers

We are
Sitting down in the dark in the days to come

Your lungs burn with sorted smoke
Leftovers imported by a book on a plane
And that empty and unendurable train

With wants wanting to endure
Packed we were and without breath
Cross country crushed cigarettes strained back to form
Lit without rush
So solid in the *then*

In those days
When the lime tree was idolatrously intact
And scents competed for our attention
I was the lover of every limitation
For first things never really last

Little girl hope is down the line
The beloved is still the beloved

And the lover could never pay the heavy fine

Languished
Waning and without a sign
Come clear North Star
Come holly bitter at your roots

Mythic creatures are constantly surprised to be sold
Colder imitations flow past
The past indentations
Exhausting your hold on me

LET THE WATERFALLS FALL OVER ME

Rome on a rotted bridge
Standing between two banks
My coffee denies all reflection
Your spoon topples in
Into the double and warm

My heart swallows the bells
The cathedral stands shell colored and lean
You must imagine it waxed with a woman's white

Cream foam on my nose
You are kissing it off
Finishing me with blown kisses

We are among the last things that last
Colder imitations flow past
The past indentations
Once double and warm

Long and leisured
We are

Burgeons of every ecstasy
We are

Released and un-refrained
We are
The now that never was

The perfume of a poor soul is a majestic solemnity
You are the redolent cadence
You chagrin my senses
The carillon peal
Carrion nipping at our heels

My God I have no more prayers
I evacuated them with the last prayer
Ever exhausted in you
You exhaust me

The cicadas have their corner garden
It would be easier that way
To scratch at the rocks and leave my shade
To be nothing more nor nothing less
Than the water and honey and wine that brim
Wild without denial or regret

Let the waterfalls fall over me
Anything real exists between wails
A beautiful and discordant minor key
Clings to the last inflection of your unnoticed goodbye

Give me moment that tips the scale
I have no where left to go
Your absence inaugurates a whole art of survival
Assisi lies north
More northern is an England tale

Southern Malta with collected shells and Crosses
Everything is ornate when love is simple
You called me Cait
In the *then* that claims me now

You remain in the trench
One of the invisible soldiers heaving First War guns
Fingers twitch and muscles tremor
You rent out the heaviest of threats

The past intangibility nears
With nothing forgotten and everything lost

Grey photos with the inarticulate at a distance

Your face is broad
Memory serves no other purpose
than to broaden your features

Forgive me
Your covenant is a protracted death
Your memory is a retrodict grace
Recoiling along the third person rank
Grammatical tanks misfire into the deep of each cheek
Drenched in repetition
Father you must hear my confession

Emblematic signs of good and evil
Beyond good and evil
The snake strikes
And the soldier lights a flame and laughs
Cleansing his cuts

The same old losses school us in their games
And haunt us fools
The salt has lost its savor
Renaming its taste in your wounds

Beyond Good and Evil
The dictum of sorrows
The balm of new wounds
The book of hours
No never stand down never cower
Redeem me Matter
Et Incarnatus est
In your body
In the heavy sex
In the long lines imploded with sanguine sound
This June of all Junes has rounded me down

Two fingers tone the cool waters
Mouths open and stutter
The pure arch

The voice of thy floodgates
Beyond the dictum balm and book
Never stand down never cower

OUR LADY'S REPRIEVE

Exemptions come at night behind our backs
With mild heartache so gentle and pure
That one could rob his own life and still have life
And we did
We had a little life

In those days of quiet quickening
We dined amid coarse ground pepper
So very black it pops in contrast to the sea salt

Everything should have its savor
So we taper the knives and expunge the first years
Rolling and showing the sharp and smooth
One decade shone in the sheers

Mother Mary
Is it possible for tears to know of their futurity?
The moment has come and gone
But his laughter was long

A strong haunting rallies the dead along these corridors
I want to believe in the most beautiful faces
Racing in their confession
Racing in their blushing
Race for me
The shape of my Mother Mary comes towards me
She breathes wordless words
She places the intangible with touch
She is the shiver sharp and smooth
Held I am
I am with her
With her tears leading fast to their home

Mary Mother of God
God is Christ
Christ is Man
I kiss the grit of heavenly tears
I am unprepared for your tears
The passion of Christ is a daily sacrament
I break in the forgiveness that nears

All my wants want to be forgotten
The ties come loose and trail behind
I come in from the yard and rest on my arm

Larches moan and wasps girt the hedges
These sounds wish for me
I know they do
For I wish for them and they drift lighter than wood
Without notice and with eternal disregard
Grasses float and become a substance of grace

Our Lady you have come and you are never gone
I wish I could find you and perish in your love

FAREWELL SESTINA

You are the firmament of foolish things
An uninhabitable hold hardwired
You rip the bandage clear
Life rises to the surface and survives this fear
I am caught in the cross currents cloaked in clay

Beauty beauty save the day

Wildflowers forsaken
The pottery forsaken
The stench of the gauze relieves me
Put them together on a table
Paint them as I heal
You steal the props that allow us to stand in silence
Every half-witted agony is handed on in violence

You are the very things that bat away a stern simplicity
An incomprehensible moment of beauty
Broken to perfection
By all the risks mouthed in a lilting verse

Love moves us backwards
From lips with hyssop to the high hedgerow
The retrograde Cross
The frost on spring berries
Sinless blood red drops
On the first man who carried
Our lifeless Lord
Full of life

The pansies climb hills *beyond* hills
Daring the galloping colt
And lost ecstasy of mountain snow
The Easter freeze strokes the sacramental April breeze

All things
Lilies touched with frost

My face
Blushes in your touch

Drowsy little lilies
Lost in the blood red collection

These things are dear to me
Shivering in the clean and holy air
I think you are near
Picking them for me
The color of plums from Lent to Advent

One Lenten lily touched with frost
Blushes in your touch
Lost lost in the blood red collection

Tears flatten into a robe
Cloaking our penitential regrets
The sun sets on another hill
Vague and disappointed features appear
Baritone deep
Whites of eyes prick with fear

A poor traitor no longer consolidates his grief
Still water accosts the petrified wood
Lost lost in the blood-red collection

The bright autumn atrophy spreads its love letters
In expatriated tears
You mouthe my words in the absence that nears
And descend into the slender plaint of silence

Sono nata lagrimar
Sono nata sospirir

Weep for me
Sigh for me
Fill your weight in me
Be the exotic and gentle distance
Dividing all distance

Mother Mary makes an advent wreath
Candles lit and little hands entreat
Bobbing for apples in the colliding season
Immortal we are
And for no right reason

In violation of reason
We accept the very soul of an *imprimis* pardon

Six days
On the seventh rest
Decades are made of days
Recollection reinstates a concaved breast
Hidden in a granite hymn and humbled down

You chase me and I am nowhere to be found
I am in the somewhere of a little town
With quaint shops and the story of three drowned boys
And roundabouts

The girls are lost and found
In play
They fold the caverns of age
With the sounds they make

Staking the heart's stay
Their voices compel the shame and joy
Of felled tears dumb in prayer on the altar rail

Tables made
Shadows laid by sun and shade
Starlings conquering the curves

Turned out in every ascetic resolve
It is time for failed knowledge
For the God of gods
Who suffers the *need* for His creatures

This Fall of Falls
This Autumn of all Autumns
Is a Platonic Form
An inaudible composition of passion
Conquering the sounds
Smells cadences and lulls
Of unworthy souls with open mouths

Sono nata lagrimar
Sono nata sospirir

Weep for me
Sigh for me
Take my life on your lips
Fill the forgotten in me
In my tears
In my sighs
Long and broken by the boughs

Plaques overgrown
A week's time rolled in hay
Small horses or little ponies
Material questions
Giggles straying into other perfections
A week's time
The tea tray
A spray of crisp mint
Cream and spiced scones
A week's time
Blunt as every other stone

You intrude every ounce of redeemer's passion
In the vague beginning of a new morning
In every measure of fixed and folded scenery
I ask you
Isn't this enough?

This aphrodisiac of risk burns the lips
Candied and crystallized ginger
A prying palate
Hot tea sighing in local shops
Breathless sips and sleep
Blanketed in the big deep
We are born to weep

We lean over the rail in an unfixed space
Where space is filled with space
The moon beams break the blackened lake
And form those obscure clues
Discerning the last location of good news

The wishing well's water aches
No new words commute this space

The cold sticks with salt
The salt sickens the cold
I am sold by every hope

Love lies in its embroidery
Every weave ceases to help its own continuation
Faster and faster
Masquerading your threat

Picaresque imperfections
The lighter the lovelier
Never soften the threat
Never fail to fit
Against the death mask

I make lines on your face on the soft sheets
Sun dried with Italian sun
Hung to dry
A ridiculously inefficient rail
One sheet haphazardly over the next
All after the sun

The loveliest whims pulled and snapped
Will on Will
Straightened into form

The incense after the storm
Barefoot in its fragrance
It took you on
As you take it on your nape and neck
You smell of that time of unvarnished oak or pine
Who can remember the difference in time?

You are the remembered difference
Extracted from the oil of every pastime
Signs of loss fell from yours to mine

My sorrowful sestina
With body aligned
We predict the present
In the line of loss
That fell from your body onto mine

The present was always our sign
Fully durational and never eternal
Between the hours you remain
The book of every hour unclaimed

My pathetic sorrows are trained
Teeming with heat
Rage does the sympathetic and braves your graceless remains
Only say the word and I will enter under your roof

The early morning whispers at the far corners
Of that moment in the *then*
In all its wicked causation
One could believe in the chatter of field mice
And the breaking of the ice

There is a stream
Infinitesimal and untouched
Out the back door
Down the slope
A bridge is made with our legs
Straddling over and threatening to fall
Little London Bridge on the felt of my gloves
Caught up in your arms and soaked

In all its wicked causation
One could believe that your arms could last
And never bow to the soft passing
When the consent of time comes home

The morning's whispers strain to see you
And resolve these depths in your face
Framed you are
Ever framed in me
By the stalled windowsill

I am the repeated drama of the little things
One spread makes me fast for Spring

The Everlasting Man lives among elected silence
Medicines dissolve
Clay hardens
Sins are absolved though faith is not magic
We are never the same forgiven souls
Before the need for forgiveness

The voice in forgiveness is and is not our own
It is not our own
As we pardon we too are pardoned every single time
For it is not our own
The one who forgives is always in debt
We are never our own
We use what we lack in order to receive what we lack
This love is and is not our own

My sheltered sestina forgive me
Forgive me with flowers on the grave
Forgive me with little things

My Lady of Grace
You persist through all identity
My Lady of Hope
Persistence is not the same as an essence
My Lady of Sorrows
Persistence unmakes essence
My Lady of Victory
I have never seen an essence
My Lady of Patience
I want to believe in what we coddle at night
My Lady of Perpetual Help
I believe my wants should not want to be forgiven
My Lady of Sad Countenance
Forgive me

Refrain
We are in the house
Where every window
Every corner
Every torn and covered chair
Every unfixed faucet
Every shade and muse is the same
And music reigns
Reigns in the pitfall

The snows of last winter
Have gone where your memory goes
Even the slowest snowflake
Escapes the divinity braiding young hair
And asking for my faith

A fugitive wind slips past the trees
I am among the sounds it makes
And the firs it touches
In these trenches
I straddle the vacuous presentiment
Exhausted by anticipation

Refrain
In this house
Where every king is the same
You are the prints on the plate
The porcelain plate on the mantle
The nails that assure the wood
The lasting endurance of a century
Where we stood silent as one

You are the elusive image of an image
In the vision of God
Chasing me
Your breath slips past my voice
Calling for you in sleep
And asphyxiates the trees

Your unshaven face
Shoots me out of immanence
Long sighs walled in
In the *then* as it never was
You make my cheeks red

Too soon
Too soon
We've become an abyss around the fire

As hollow as the belt that loops around
And does the feeling for me and for you
It is all too soon

My Lady of Grace
The water may be enough
The life promised after this life
Is nothing like the water

Promises are not enough
With all the risks I tighten my scope
I regret my God and ask for water over life

Forgive me
I am not worthy to enter under your roof
In the one act of faith
In ruthless love
I give back my ticket

In ruthless love
I give back my ticket

Under your roof
Within your face
Hastening your Being
I give back my ticket

My Lady of Hope
Is the lightest and the loveliest
The exotic and gentle distance
She loops around and does the feeling for me

Baptize this soul hanging in harmony and strife
My hope weakens the leftover hold
Fallen face down
I keep persisting against your grain

Abysses call forth the abyss
Give me over and do not hesitate
Bring me over the fire
And burn the life out of me

LIGHT OF ALL VALLEYS, LIGHT OF ALL FACES

My God
If you still hear my prayers
I pray for duration
For flickering candles along limestone walls
Light of all valleys
Light of all faces
Bring me over the fire
Burn the life out of me

Your fable
Your blood red rose
Your rose has my blood
A crown of thorns
To dip in
You take me on with every nail
You dig into me
You pull substance from the ashes
You cross every path and take away these sins

Seasons have their sacrilege
They change our perpetuation
They uproot our flowers
They recoil within us

In the presumed happy ending
In the *then* that never was
Goodbye kisses are so utterly human
Poisoned on immortality
I ask you
Isn't the dropping summer sacrament enough?

Last things hit the tin and make a thud
You accompany me
A good soldier

Through every pulse and pain

Recollections on melting snow
Little flowers and little leaves
All the virgins of nature
Posthumous under the elms

My God dearly I love you
If you still hear my prayers
I pray for dried tears
Now pooling on his handkerchief

In the mutiny of every fallen knee
Layers upon layers in every martyred tree
Little we are in the littleness we own
Light of all valleys
Light of all faces
Isn't this enough?

Clover leans along the lane
I believe I feel your lips
I bow and hush and ask for you
To make these cellars sane
Sing to me in a slow tongue
Bring me over the fire
And burn the life out of me

Dripping rain
The sound of vespers unscathed
The sickle slants and casts its scythe
Dropping grasses disorient the dew
And inaugurate
The long homing coo
And you
You are enough
With unended mortal roots

Floating for an instant
Grasses glow golden
And insist on casting a spell
Over you
Cutting the azure
Cursing the plains
Under and through
The sidling green
And you
You are enough
With unended mortal roots

I am I
For the kill
In the instant
Before the knife pulls
The thorn pulls
You pull from inside me
With unended mortal roots

The tulips flood with color
In a Spring's first pull
The final pull disrupts the soil
For a body of time
You lay on me and remind me of what a soul can do

What is heard is heard only with selection
Light of all valleys
Light of all faces
Isn't this enough?

We locate the rounded river stones
You have kept to that tone
You fasten a low soul to an empty throne

What sighs
Sighs only with selection
Light of all valleys

Light of all faces
Isn't this enough?

Lost things in a forgery of essences
You hasten a low soul to an empty bed
One valley
One face

You had your northern neglect
I had my books
A pile of last things cluttered a corner desk
One valley
One face

New York in black and white
Shades bless the sky
The day is sent to night
One valley
One face

And I beg you, Isn't this enough?

Refrain
One soul singing in the sold house
Where window bodies look longer than life allows
You thicken into every pulse

In a low alley
Your imposter stings fast
Dipping into the dark grapes and glass bowl
Dipping through the portos and cupolas of the Umbrian hills

Touch is the forgotten transcendental
Paved over with Roman cobbles
Utterly human and resignedly rare
This dropping Summer sacrament is enough

Sorrento is close

Nearby lemons
Falling overripe from trees

Again
You have a close shave
Citrus leaves oversized
Green and shiny with wax
A perfect contrast

Again
Your face reddens my cheeks
Disapproving kisses kiss me again!

Fermented globed delicacies
Your lips wrap where there is no pit
We are in a garden
With accents and nothing bare
Pull up a chair

On that clay painted serving tray
Packed so carefully
Creation re-creates everything aside from time

An exigent thought takes us to the short side of perfection
Forgive our lover's sin
Love needs our un-guarded shins
And shining imperfections

Your crooked teeth
Their dents hit me
Take me and take me down
Take the third chair
We need only these and these stone stairs
And these canopy trees
And these stars where stars expire

In the now as it never was *then*
Nothing holds those passing positions

And feigned careless airs

Refrain
Hands dwindle down below the bramble
A sunset between two chairs
Under the table's edge
The lover's imperfection
Neither skin nor tablecloth could share

Wood above us
Grass below
Sky and time
Time and sky
Knotted and rough
The glass fell unbroken on tender grass
A perfected alchemy
Invincible to the bees

My sorrowful sestina
Stretched over nothing
Making nothing
In arcadia ego
Acadian honey and forgotten ghosts

Words could not eat away at us
We forgot how they were drawn and crossed
Forgotten in their in-between passageways
Their narrow little alleys
Running from collection

The *danse macabre* of our little death
Is furthered in foreign fear
Put your hands on my hips
And on my face
Sear the edges of the paper
Fire black and brittle
Rapes the light lace
All actions and innocence ended

In this thy hour of Grace

Neglected postures knead the dough
Crisp apples and brown burning drinks
And you are near
You are the nearness imbued in sunset silence
Silent shades and ships
Shelters and rain
Virginal rain on closed eyes

You are these reasons *beyond* reason
One solitary and banished
Late afternoon presence wafting in the sirocco
A shared slip of sighs
Rye fields harbors and moons
Lay the land for penance and prayer

Carry me farther than desire
Into the land of early myth
Far-fetched I am and in the rain
Perfect rain
Rain
Perfect and momentary rain

You are the highest poverty
The verity of nothing
Lift the veil of my foreign sorrow
And cover me with your life
My life is on your lips
In the beginning and in the end
Let me remember what a soul can do

From the crescent to the full stare
Slow yourself down to a dull sound
Ducking into my dark door
I make out the tent of trees
And the Mass in B minor

Et Incarnatus est
Crucifixus
Et Resurrexit
Let me remember what a soul can do

Wood doors
Cherry stained in Oxford accord
Frame your face in a decade of past dues
Ancient and aging ruse come down to me
Let me remember what a soul can do

Your face is an image of an image
I imagine your pace fastening through the scenes
Backing through the hollow stone arches
Bitten through with illumination in my shade

I am passing over you
In the sold soul
In the séance of a forged essence
I can no longer afford

The burnt tears ensue
And the man has come through
What an exquisite chisel
Chiseling through
Christenings dig trenches down my cheeks
And into the deep of my neck
Where you hide and I seek

AD MEMORIAM AETERNAM

Amber tones mock the ceiling
Hoarding these tiresome shadows
I come restless and with bitter lips

Nevermore colludes with you in quiet despair
Fjords further your frightful and static path
I come hollowed and with bitter lips

I thought I felt you come in
The sun fails to sink in
Transparent and teething in this likening block
I come full of thirst and with bitter lips

In eternal memory
In perpetual disregard for the staff and rod
With the voice of thy floodgates
With every bend of our humiliated God
Turn my insides out
And bring the turn-sister of hope home

Hit me with wine
With water
With warmth
With every parochial innocence
I come with abandonment to divine providence
And with the bitterest of lips

The time is Lent
Of nearing lateness
Dark nights
And coarse Lenten cloth

Long revolting reeds
Fingers amid smoke

Yellow at their tips
I come before the gaze of divine countenance
And with the bitterest of lips

Every memorial is scented with the chatter of next of kin
Scattering heaps of hope and new tints of life
The sounded din of the dinner bell
Finding hands
Husbands and wives
Little lives
Little lives
As we were *then*

There are roses against your gate
The grate needs fresh paint
I pass through
Remembering what a soul can do
Forgetting what a soul can do

In a future risk
The man will come through
Roses you said banish us to the dead
One mortal faith
One mortal hope
On the grave of mortal love

Silence spreads its laces
For some other sweetness ahead
Forget what is ahead
Shed your clothes and wash this stone

Petals drenched in your salt
Still savoring the salt
The red is let in
You smell like life
For a moment in time
Harmony subdues this strive

The last Christian died on the Cross
For a moment
In time
In a decade to forsake
The turn-sister never late
Lay down your abstractions
Light footed on the light frost

You come home
Still cleaning in a patter and rush
Still a handful of dust
Still adorning the easy corner
Stillness steals us at every corner
Where every king is the same

ET ERRAVERIT UNA EX EIS

You are
The stillness between a body
Pulled limb from limb
You are that kind of grace

You are
The myths making haste
On my mouth and on my teeth
With the dead and with the bitterest of lips
Your forgiveness hits every bone
One by one
Inaugurating the eternal art of survival

Take back the grey wisps behind your ear
Where are the snows of last winter?
Where are the last years?
Take back your calm hand amid late Lenten tears

My sorrowful sestina
I am not worthy to remember what a soul can do
But you press on
You press these things
These infinitely kind infinitely cradling things

Ancient words and ancient forgiveness
Miles forged in forgiveness

Sic non est voluntas
Ante Patrem vestrum qui in caelis
Est ut pereat unus de pusillis istis

When one goes astray
The Father leaves none behind
Lost lambs unable to pay the fines

Patience in these lost lines
Patience in these soft signs
Psalmist rhymes and vineyard rows
Window life comes and goes
Body and blood
The pure and irresistible *elan*
Long and strong
Selfless and ruthless you are
Forgive our sins
Forgive our need

Only make the sign and we shall be forgiven
Forgiven in love
Forgotten debts
Remitted debts
As Fathers can give to sons
As the Father gave his Son

And we forget
With debts remitted
We forget
With debts remitted

Your love is inscrutable
The absurdity of pure causation
The joy and fear waking the first sensation
Inescapable and suffering
You bow your head
Thumb under eye
And wiped across the cheek
Such a beautiful fool
Quixote patterned after you

You are the inescapable ruin
The end of all causes
The unendingly gentle lover
You bow your head for the other
Again and again

And without notice
We forget
With debts remitted
We forget

REMEMBER ME CONTRA MUNDUM

Sacks of surprises
The kitchen door
Always in
Warmer *then*
Hot from the oven
Worth every percussion it sends
The salmon pink past raw
As warm as wine

The basil crushed with golden garlic
A rough tongue and tawny oil
A cold pressed port
Again I bought the cold water lobster
Disapproving kisses kiss me again
Your chin drips in lover's sin
It tastes of plum cherubs and sweet pulp

You bolt down my thighs
The second round of laughter
Sends laughter and laurel into the next room
In the stillness won with affectionate lungs
You take a deep breath and take me in

In Easter
In Mary's blossom time and berry time
The radiant appearance of the eternally non apparent
Snaps the winter's grace
A patch of green spars with another hue
Ad infinitum springs anew

Amid the half finished woodworks
Cast off pots
Supplanted garden tools
And shredded grey wool

The furious finitude of early love
Returns to break the boughs

We overcame need and eternity
In the duration that was our own
In secret procession
We overcame the other
Till the ends of the earth
Till the ends of the earth
That spanned across a face
In the doubt that could not catch up

Most lilies are the wisest of white
But these oriental beauties are insurmountably pink
The sink's edge
Stems cut
Thin raw bones balance at the brink
Cracks for a time on porcelain lips
White as the divide on our Father's collar
A rim of water with one frail shield
Running through the duration that was our own

In your shoulders
In the very presentiment of bondage
Into its prefigured lateness
A fire
A summer festival
Smolders alongside your low strung cigarette
So careful you are
You are life between graces

On the beach rimmed in darkness
Passive purification strips the senses
And then the soul
A stone's cacophony
Burrows into our blind balcony

Wax wet and half past its first form

Blown papers litter the ground
So careful you are
You are life between graces

In the carelessness of blossom time
And berry time
We are the failed witnesses
With nothing more and nothing less
Than a shred of finder's grace

Let the reprieve sing through the hills

We lay like lazy lovers
Watching celestial prophecies
The television blinks
The odd couple
The same story
Thumbing through the power and the glory
Kindling our spirits

You put candles on
Honoring secret Madonnas
Quiet Josephs with long shade
Feel our glow
In the *now* never *then*
No act of contrition
Could bring us back again

I am a tyrannical little child
With all the lacks
Contra mundum
Contra naturam
Sed contra
I curse all the facts

I am younger than my time
More wild than the wildest winter
Beating ice on ancient glass sanded with lead

Sounds in a thicket burst the landmine
In the time of first weeping
I begin to weep

I find my life on hyssop-stung lips
From the strangeness of distant pain
To the nails lodged *ad aeternam*
On crossed feet and hands
The scent of roses rise from broken graves
Incorruptible remains
I find my way within His tears
In the persisting grace pulled year from year

Mother Mary
Could your solemnity compare to the steep tread
Raising hell down my sides?

Our Lady
Eternal Mother of the infinitely gentle
Infinitely suffering child
Forgive me
Forgive me for what a question hides
Emptier than Christ's sides
Blood of nothing
Blood of life
I rely on the dead man's lot of lies

I come with nothing to give and with the bitterest of lips

Our Lady of Atonement
I have nothing left but changing hates
As empty as the rules of fate

God of my love
God abandoned
Where have I gone after having gone through you?

Lady of my Lips

Lady derided
Where have I gone after having gone through you?

Christ of my tears
Christ denied
Where have I gone after having gone through you?

Through the ghost
The flesh
The body
The blood

Nothing breaks the boughs like love
Nothing but love
Condemns us to our mortality

At the second fall a stranger picks up the Cross

Ahead and behind
Sacral arches from a shell
A cabernet colored cathedral
You yell to me with urgency and life
Catching me as I go away

Your voice pounds through me
At the station of the second fall
Strangers record distance
With distance renamed
Make the sign of the Cross
In this heavy loss
Nothing breaks the boughs like love

Your voice beats me out like bronze
Catching me as I go away
Framed by the arches in June
Brutal and unreliable thoughts
Waste away in the ringing bells

Grey sticks brick on brick
My prayers finished miles before yours
I wait for you in the dark and thick
I think of strawberries freshly picked

Re-visitation remains hollow
Escapism in the fire
Little seeds bleed between teeth
A melismatic hold in a dreaming spire

A single sin tenders its reach
And swallows the length of this half-wit soul
I dot the four places
With water from a clear bowl

Refrain
A stranger carried the Cross
At the second fall
A plaque against the wall
In the house
Where two thin lines intersect
And nothing is the same

NON SUM DIGNUS CALCIAMENTA PORTARE

In the anticipation of the birth of our Lord
In the startled vastness of light glinted seas
In the curve of infant lips
You press on
You press these infinitely gentle
Infinitely suffering things

Static charms
The darning and the eight fifteen
Auden knew of a dotted farm
Parceled perfection in all the shivers of Spring
Fir trees prepared for the half year
With wit and warm light and early cheer

The choir's eyes align
And breathe the unnoticed nascent sigh

The winter tires into Spring
It carries the secret stillness in time
To tire into Fall

Autumn mittens with painted pumpkins
Smiles around the table
Worm wood knots traced with little fingers
Soft peach to passion flesh
Sweet things carved into the passing calm

You surround me with lilac and straw wine
The sun on the manger
Estranges the strayed collection
Incredulous belief upends every beginning with an end
And every end with wisdom beginning again

A winter's psalm brings about the *then*
Light footed in the tenth year
Carried with corseted tomes and neutered tense
Nothing more nothing less than *consummatum est*

A specter of suspicion
Condemned my arms and knees
I fell into the maker's lament
Knowing neither its depths
Nor the soul
Nor the body
That withstands silent confession

All remains have poor timing
Catching and spreading themselves
Through the veins of each pine
Life by the evening train
A wail and wearied sign
Tracks have backward glances
Quickening lines and loaded stares

Fated and forgotten
A fool amid foolish things
Dismiss all universal causes
And smugly clean determinisms
For my wants want to be forgotten
Nothing more nothing less than *consummatum est*

Our Lady
Nothing carries on
All facts destroy themselves
Not long after the dawn
You alone brave their remains
Re-arranged within your Son

Our Lady of Victory
Sweet virgin
Life of *eros*

Life of all surrender
My wants do want to be forgotten

I am a whimper
A flying essence
I want to end in Him
My innocence must be cunning
I want to end in Him

God of three persons
Forsaken
In Thoughts
In Words
In Being
Divide the last divisions
I want to end in your boughs

Here we stay
Here is where the half past three
Sacrificial ritual raids the cupboards

As the fields dissipate
As grasses are leaned out
As cold water and clusters of hops are made golden

    Here is where stained glass grazes its touch

Within every turn where larches bloom
Your love divides the indivisible
Suffering for me
You feed your roses to their thorns
And free me for your grace

NOVITIATE GRACE

A violet colored fruit
In your byzantine mouth
The penitential thrust enters and
You grow with that kind of grace
Pulled limb from limb

The loveliest lavender is spent
Dancing in the dark ages
Distributing alms down our throat

The season of somber
Begins in the night wanderer's song
Where nothing is new
And nothing is let loose

I hold on through this death
You press your tongue interred
I invite myself down
We share the same blood
Pretending its blood
Like fleas
We are
Already conquering the divide

The skin is breached
You reach for wildflowers
And rise past honeyed moons
In the innocence of pure resolve
Nothing is new
And nothing is let loose

Your skin confesses all my false hopes
Unshaven and half dead

Coarsely rubbing against my breasts

You begin the distance
That makes the saint
That makes the dead

Fingers slope like antlers
On a raised edge
Kissing me with hard lips
I am uncertain of everything
Except the brief strain on sun white linen
And your hard lips softening over my face

You are bitter
You are kind
You are every infinitely suffering thing
You have begun the distance
That makes the saint
And breaks the dead

Your Pascalian wager
Writes a work of tears down my face
On my chest
Through my thighs
Past my feet
Your touch leaves without notice
This life has taken away my escape
You have begun the distance
As I lunge to return

Martyrs and lovers carry a coda of the Passion
Decades and seasons carry a coda of the Passion
Rain perfect and momentary rain
I stand still
The marrow of relics carries a coda of the Passion
I am unprepared for your years
Forgive this novice
Forgive what a soul can do

I TELL MYSELF WITH A JEALOUS LOVE

New England pumpkins rush us through the lore
In the *then* the hills have cooled down
Low slung sacraments
Line a tinker's town

Strands record your face
The frost patterns the sestina
You are immortalized in slow motion

Still trees close around us
And then vigorously shake
Back down I imagine
Back down they say

Slaves to Brutus
Slaves to Rome
Slaves to mortal hope
And past presentiments
Laying low

We thank the gods that Crane found rest
And the country became one
Such fools we are and foolish things
Lay low for us
Lay low

Laughter laughing after the fact
We carved kindness into light
Holiness in the passing flesh
Holiness comes in childlike change
Lay low for us
Lay low

The failed logic
The logic of perfection
A constructed *kathodos*
Wrapped in a decade
Stalled with a bliss
And our Lady's kiss

Lay low for us and in us
Lay low

Such a soul as I am now
Is too tired to fail
The frail sensuality of the evensong hits its pitch
And carves me with its light

Voices at the floodgate
                    Never drop your voice
With age and its neglect
                    Never drop your voice

Two shoulders show me the way to bed
Night clouds have their own bed of colors
Under the covers you wear me out
Lay low in me
Lay low

The floors creak
We tread
You follow faster into the rafters
Floating red locks
In the rafters
Faces go down
Heavy as lead
In a mercury slip
You slide in

The leak from the sink
Uncared and unfixed

Transfuses the cricket's sound
The creed of the lover
Was never so loud
Lay low for us
Lay low

I am an elected silence
A stone dotting towards the gate
I lay low with you
Against the world
Against nature
On the contrary
And without the facts

Denying the evening by being the night
The leaves are resplendent
We weep for the seasons
And the meaning of shadows
The essence of gratuity follows us through death
Lingering dark lakes extend through the closing door

These foolish things remind me of you
I think of Christ's Passion
I dare not hope for our resurrection
Our wounds are cut red
In the *now* as it never was *then*
I lay low with you
Against the world
Against nature
On the contrary
And without the facts

On that promenade in a New York June
Heated summer spells fill the borough of Brooklyn
Crane and Whitman bowed to the bridge
Bowing and commuting our sentiments
From Willow, Cranberry, Remsen and Bayridge

From Cobble Hill
And Anglican glass and said Mass
You break the boughs
You are the infinitely sweet infinitely suffering soul

In the *now* that passes lovers
We walk like lovers
Because for the moment
Ella sings her Foolish Things
Seven minutes of a song
Resurrect two empty bodies

I love you
When the gardenia
And its perfume hits the pillow
Right after the first daffodil
Reminds us of the first spring

How strange and sweet it all was
After the world
After nature
After the fact
In the contrary that denies its completed solemnity

Today I saw you weep
With shallow tears
Tears too weak to defeat me
As I turned to the road

Hunger was no longer there
And tastes no longer ravished

You are dying the gentle death for me
You are doing it so politely

You terrorize me with your kind regard
What a fool you are
What foolish and miserable things

You sing to me

How these things are dear to me
I breathe the burned out cathedral again

Seeds pulled from the deep pumpkin
Are once more in your hands
A mess covers my face and we play
In a decade too deep in the *then*

You begin to die the gentle death
And you do it so politely

Martyrdom for lovers begins in a song
Innocence collapses in the agonic refrain

Everything breathable and adaptable to hope
Kills in its touch
Love is an evil too good for home
I cannot taste the sugar or the frost

I have combed the black sands
And nothing less than nothing
Hits me with its shape

Adamant hands plant life
I see the cherub trees
The juniper's spindly leaves prick me
I taste their blue berries curing some future ailment
I smell the bitterest of chocolate streamlining my cup

Inanimate creatures break their bonds
I imagine they long with God
The anticipation of opening roses
Cascade like lovers against the grain
Along the marches
Birds bathe in holy rain

In recollection
Let us not add another rhyme
Nor another perfection
But it is true
There was a tiny lissom lane
And lovely fruits that feed the sheep

We pulled them apart like the flock
And popped them in our mouths
Plush to fade in our mouths
Perfect tastes in our mouths
One substance in your mouth and mine

The ghosts of substance and shadow
Tried to save the present in the past
Nothing less than nothing lasts
And still you call this Friday Good

I see a ship streamlined by the sun
Such a brilliant white
No such color could compare to the *then* of this white

Snows in a country house
Where deer would feel at home

Light linen sheets
Cooling us and salvaging our regrets

Whiter than the sides of your eyes
Where I am now
In the gaze of a panting God
Prior to His last word

I tell myself with a jealous love
That there is nothing more perfect than Christ
And it is He whom you love
You love Him for me

I hear your voice along the floodgates
Sensuous and certain
The lime tree blossom
The form of a quiet stage

You press into me
That simple perfection
You remind me that in Christ alone
We suffer the most pure form of Love

You remind me of these infinitely gentle
Infinite suffering things
With forgotten wants
You want me to love Him
You die the gentle death for me
You do it so politely

You are that kind of grace
Whiter than white
Darker than darkness

I could never look through you
I am along the peripherals
Where the sun splits to night

The room is little and white
A dusky white with wires
My sin is the comfortable sin
I am taken in
I care for nothing
For there is nothing more
Than the song of a forgotten soul
Forgotten by its own flesh

Nothing less than nothing
Whiter than white
Darker than darkness

I am the poor separated soul
That clings like breath on lips
Fearful of the world foreign to your touch

The air so foreign
If it is not breathed in by you

I am the silly little lamb lost in the woods
A sad and sheltered conflict
A counterfeit redeemed
Oceans redeemed
Motives redeemed
Steam ships smoke and fog
I wipe away your face on mine

Nothing less than nothing
Whiter than white
Darker than darkness
You are that kind of grace

I read your books
I smell your cloth
Your pictures before my time
I read how the soul and the body
In their addition
Deny addition and become one
I make your vigil on New Year's Day

In Mary's solemn way
I become the sweet suffering thing I love
I find my time
Glass Latin candles
Seven days before Grace
In every July
In every winter
In every July
I come home

Hunters redeem the hunt with the rod and time
Lengths unseen break with the rod and time
Older than my age
I have begun to feel older than my age

Love's disproportionate perfection
Rapes the edge
And leaves only the sap of the thorn
I wipe away your face on mine

You are the enduring either/or
The tyrannical forgiveness
Betraying me in all my recollections
I wipe away your face on mine

Nothing less than nothing
Whiter than white
Darker than darkness
I close my eyes
The bright corn and hay lay fodder at your gate

You are the setting soul
You are the kiss that shames itself
You are the edge of penance
You are that kind of grace

SUMMA SOLEMNIS

Que ton absence soit une nouvelle figure de ton etre a jamai senti; ton ineffable depart, sure amie, inaugure tout un art survie.

—*RAINIER MARIA RILKE*

AD PRIMUM: ET UMBRA MORTIS

"That which has been is now ..."

It is as if we could depart faithfully
From this loving leap of blood and time
Pressing cold upon our faces
Mingling deep in the receding waves
Looking for the hold to complete our frames
Burrowing amongst the stones of throw
One could not let go
Let be
Let slow
But held so in the sleight of hand curled
And embalmed within the scrolling foam

Muddling my words in your mouth
Now opened to the gleam of night
Moon frames your smile
Sides pierced and run dry
Never mind this flood where we have bent our backs
Turn in its grandeur
Turn more upon the naiveté
That swimming lifts all souls above the fire

Last love in the lumen of Grace
In the shake before the standstill
In the making of the nightingale
In its wings evaded by truth
In the crestfallen gestures that mothers make
When the womb cannot take

Such things that are good happen early
Happen soon into the dew
Into the ground
Into the frame for which I knew

My love would not be made even

Anticipation rounded forth from the loss of presence
Grappling for a hold against the waves
Lapping staggering recesses
Lashings under lashings disavowed

Love comes to haunt
To come back in bruised form
To have and to behold
To fold with greater force than before
In spectering form I tremble against the brace

God save thee from these open plays that place the hand upon the jaw
And wish the tremor would not be the Fall
Make penance for flowers against the wind

These are thy relics sent on rescue missions
Lace lined hints of smells long sheltered and dried
A tattered letter
A prayer in a foreign tongue
Bruised with nothing more than coarse cut tears
Prayers after prayers after patterns after you
Long after words

Far along the laurels and amidst the dew
You lead me against hope
Winding staircases shone slick in the newness gone by
Remnants of a distant bloom fill the air
Disconsolate and chastened creeks choke and sigh

Fallen into the fray of a lonelier aftermath
What may come of these less than divinized hands?
What could appease this doom?
It resurrects all fronts against your pacifying speed
This corpse and its tyrannical need has only hatred
Hatred for the ends creation must maintain and seize!

Ease this hold in sterling clutches upon the bell
I held and held as they sang
Blood rang from my ears
In recollection of the kill
Savage tears still the lungs
Till it was yours and mine
Entwined in this blissful absence of space
Sunken into the recesses of eyes without sleep
Twist at the prospect of knowing enough blame not to care
To care less than before
To weep in ignorance and shame
To weep for love that can no longer make lame

Shapes fail form and reflect their barren cues
As it was mine *in time* in yours *in time*
One touch more
And one touch less
No never meeting to confess
The requisite regard
All is guarded and derided

Lay low in the garments of a virgin Spring
Drop into the background and refrain
Thy newer shades will never confess what was required or regarded as
   required

Reified by these visages of shape
Traipsing upon the inscapes of arms and knees
Savagely pressing so lightly in fear
In the recompense nature of my early year
Years upon years
Wounded in the ways of mortal men
Bound my being in sinful thanksgiving.
In graceless relief lie lesser goods
Calling on lesser gods and gods unknown
I kiss the bees that stung upon your mouth

My little one of frightful sums

Delighted and dead
Unrequited and done
Why have you spent your charity on my lacking?
More than apathy alone curls fingers to the palm

Against lesions laced on feet
I dragged my longing
Its salt on flesh to flood the face
To this once crucified end
I moved with gripping
I moved with single thoughts
Movement ceases in the sway
It covers your hands with forgotten stains
It stems across the shadowlands of your demise
And then bleeds forth upon the surprise
That you had me all the time

God pray for your creature
Prayers to undo this wanting prayer
For the reciprocity of forget
Frozen in the lyre raw stems
For which my heart growls
Against its lonely discord

Frail hands intersect
The weaving of muscles upon your back
Reflexes recall the lashing
Where love stigmatized your soul
You've grown melancholy
In my dangerous clutch
In my repentance that must be done

Fallen shards cascade their blooms along your fall
And winter springs an even call
And what about summer you say
Of French paired reds
And sailboat parties
And canopies yellowed

Under the early evening sun

Dare to remind in daggered crush
Come with me
And be a lousy scavenger of the mind
Break the back of this organ
And expire its thoughts
Its purse against the storm
Neglect the fruition that finds its recourse in the shade
Fade too soon in the forgery that spares Joy
As it forages for a stay

Little trees in a thicket
Glistening in rain
I am drunk again on sap and other such souls
I have gagged for sun against the gashes on the floor
Little undertow beats back
The school of fish
Circling in resolute accord
Forgive me
I am the daggered crush
Whimpering along the breaks

Creeks bare their banks like teeth
Folding rivulets of sand down their sides
I do not know nor can I say
I cannot be so easy and so free
Sing to me after the press upon your hold
Numb my being with your loving scold

One song to reach its end
One song is all I ask
One song to leave the leaves aligned
Flustered across our corpse of time

Lull to sleep this greed
This hope
spent on mornings

When rain prevents the day from coming
Huddling swiftly to a standstill and drawn in
Before the color set in and bled

Dead leaves play out their discourse
Eluding the vandal underfoot
Their rise and fall mimic the strange wail of vespers
In their veiled tears
I long for the littlest to ensue
For a glimmer upon the divide
Never mind day or night
Give over something to Name
Some secret so miserably perfect
Imperfectly beautiful that it strips the Lenten grey
And begs for a stay with each bruise upon the heel

Strange ground finds insteps unsoiled by time
Furnishing knees fallen in kind
Pressed to the spine of this uncertain hill
Tread and fear in mutual rhyme
Find compromise for an early year
Another early autumn

Little girl so tired of it all
Of the call to bring back beauty welling from eyes
The sea is a virtuoso that comes hither and plays
Rocks nestle in tiny shoes worn clear of their gleam
It is everything and nothing that I have known
But it is mine kept away from the spine and shift
That will not obey the seamless line
You call me for my joy
But I am troubled to know what saves us
From the making of alone
Tell me what can be undone!

Kisses summon honeysuckle
And unhinge the agony of thy penitent stare
Bees border along ridges

And hiss through plum vine lips
Swollen in loss so pure so dead
Give me presence in this absence of divide
Give me immanence in your transgressions
As they are mine
Place your thoughts in my eyes
For natures are to be forgotten.

Recollection of earlier days
Shallower in hallowed graves
Hallowed in shallow graves
Turned out and tilled by forgiven sins
Turned more in the bend
The dancer bends
Tension bristles between the body of Being and blood
Things leave and remain un-soothed
All along the way of spiraling decay
I am forbidden to move

I will fail you my love
If love depends upon my failure
I will fail in the curve of your neck
I will fail to recognize your death
In the folding of hands upon the flesh
I will fail to move as it draws near
As it draws its blood upon my lips
Let it withdraw its sacrament from my failure to remain
I will not fail this end
I will move past ends
I will fail the beginning by denying the end
One body
One Flesh
One Blood
I will fail these ends
To the ends of the earth that span across your face
To the ends that unearth such a gentle rape

I would trade my eyes that scan warm along these hills

Dappled things that Hopkins saw
Such things cut me caught in the coarse cut
I would trade my eyes
For your scent again
Fine things wilted across a wooden table
They never die
They are the dying

Please give over
These organs from which I breathe sponge blood into my mouth
Filled with honey and the egg and the matter for which we feed upon
You have left me in the hunt when I should be done

Repetition ceases in the same sorrow that brings you near
Closer than the fear of regret
Closer until proximity stills
I have treaded there all along
So close that I cannot feel the trembling that now consumes
Solemn summaries such as these

I am the intolerable ruin soaked in your memory
that mounting cloth filled with the oil of fine cut phantoms
Christian tears, I have none
but a tear of Christ, I am
I am not I
I am the ghost
I am your flesh
forgive me
you can no longer fade from my sight
your tears are a menace against my cheek
your face
 they drain into
your mouth
they roil another work of silence
I am among the tears of Christ
I'll look for you as I wash my feet

Scratch against the abyss

And etch a small existence for you and me
Follow the things that come again
Pass away like lovers in sway
Pray to be burned and blessed

Give over
And under
Forget direction
And forgive time

Tell me about the things that can be undone
Lay there with your fears so pure
So never misspoken
Fall asleep as laughter intoxicates another room
And drifts down the hall
Sheets diaphanous and pitiful
Lithe and unassuming
Cover the blind as they seek the sun

Betray all words of our kind
Lines interest and remind
Make the sign of the Cross and fall under
Into the cool
Spark the chill that laments nothing but what it has forgotten

Waters wander and rail against the knots
The great particular
The great unsought
a consummate failure loaded the deck
A scant stillness washed the face
Among these things
Among these thoughts
The sound of vespers never stopped
Caught in the strange leisure
That rallies like lead
And draws out the petals staining the pool
The unfathomable certainty of waters and the shake of grace
The brutal fold on fold

The shake of little girls trembling with wings in their hands

Careful when placing distance between the over
The under and the debts unacknowledged
From the kneeler to the long birch
In this loan and in this night
We huddle in its lonelier exhaustion
Prayers of little girls tremor in space
Up and down we pace between repose and response
Knowing not how to respond

I know neither hope nor dread
Only the shape of your lips
Overflowing and unfed
Anthems dissipate and dismay
Scents cloy and betray
The will is imperfect
The will is the sacrificial plain
Easily torn
Highly arched
Closed to the vision of the sky
Beyond fear
Beyond the break
Beyond good and evil
I was wrong all along

Forgive my inability to repent
Prescribed in occasions like these
In situations of undoing proximity
When hissed lips are pulled with blinding force
And maddening glory

I know neither hope nor dread
Only the shape of your lips
As they are mine
For I have forgiven direction
And forgotten time
And some other sin along these lines

Sing outside agony and sigh in slumber
And stumble over innocence again
The soft skinned child knows no anguish of his innocence
Let him sleep unknown to the hours longing
Let him lull longer than recollection

The brooding hum kisses with its splendor
And now your touch retains its wait
There is nothing more
Nothing left for us but lost anticipation
That last measure of added defeat

Forgiven sins never disengage from time
They lie in union with our fears
And ease me towards the rose
Branded with the ethereal
Quieted and coveted by the mire

Your soul is in my mouth
Your life is on my lips
Your hands upon my breast
Time moves bodies
My hips upon your face
The window is barely large enough for air
Bodies move time
The tip of tongue applies pressuring words
And resolves itself into its dark night

God grant my love a Lover's death
Leave me flamed and impassioned by fear
But give him the passion of the calm
End it all
So that all that remains conciliates my failure to remain.

AD SECUNDUM: MORTALITAS ET CARITAS

I give to you my undivided regret
A simpler anguish without regard for its consecration
Or for those other unspoken things that never find recourse for their
    attention
Reality is a recluse forged in this furnace below
We never had anything to show
Dangling toes knock upon the wishing wells of sin
Trace and lead and never heed this uncertain end
Distraction thickened around my mouth
Words can no longer penetrate only facilitate
The growl of little death that enchants in its decay
That spirals like the river bends
Bewilders the clay-framed divine and then signals
That *then* had passed like crimson softening in the snow

Fists of uncompromising penance
Stay to repeat the loss of blood
This body is a lost foe
Found in the fall of single-handed remorse
Nothing is held evenly in this dignified fallacy
Nothing escapes the tinged hue of candles
Strewn in far off churches
In far lost lands

Forgiveness and guilt clasp hands like little girls
Magnificently unprepared for that long littleness
Which ensues and burdens these ancient walls
Cold stone pressed its wine for empty eyes
For miles and miles
For rows and rows
Amber beads warm for another worn prayer
Through fingers and thumb nothing can be undone
In a stranger corner trails an oil stain more beautiful than its illusion
Her light and heavenly eyes well with resin and feverish touch

For miles and miles
For rows and rows
Empty rows quicken into miles once valid
Swarming bees bow and hush this sweet undertaking
This savor I cannot defend

Bells hollow a heavy head
That failed to position the things that should have been
Bells make passage for a stilled heart that gambles with its flutter
And flattens at the final rung
Bells along the corridor
And out into the coriander and ivy lane
A pastoral eros sinking its fragrance into the neck
All for the silent rape that recollects anticipation

Bridle this wreckage and ride without pause
Remember the sound and the sand
Remember those words without sound
And then
        Crawl in and forget what was
Place the lamb-soft fields upon your face
And chasten those thoughts against the night

Lips fill in preparation for the press
To conquer the divide of two souls separate in the pull and ply
Softer now
Beg for more overgrowth to rot this forgotten tomb
Quiet now
Leap past the balm that threatens to preserve and reciprocate time
Sunday has come again
And Sunday just the same has gone away with a leavened force

Do not think
I do not know
The cuts that could speed the way
In which the lonely feed gravity
This time forsaken line plays the lyre's raw stems

That wisp upon your face
Confuse the hand in hair
Confuse the Grace
Weep a little less
And sweep back those strands to the jaw-line curve
It turns like straws of honey gold
Pillowing down into your sight
You brush it forth never minding the flight from form
The clouds mingle and begin to suture the storm
Pandering orbs collect their reflected love and return to their wait
I mourn without object and you hesitate.

Prayers after prayers after patterns after you—long after words

God forsake regret as if lost
And never to be found
Your tyrannical forgiveness commands all pain
Bring us home along the sugar and the frost

I could never know what compelled the rain
Nor how it staged a sanctuary of minimal response
Dropping shadows christen the puddles
Giving brief passage for laughter at a close call
Your ghost censures its palpability
I have nowhere left to turn
Maudlin love
Small and uneven
Your meditations are my last rite
Burn and cool the candles from sight

A delicate haunting knocks on the door
From inseams into dreams and down onto the floor
Stirring cords have a way of moving towards the Good
And my failure is apparent in their playing
A singular move motions one step before the last call
Recognition sobers under tumbling flesh
Hands burned and mangled
Nothing more could save us now

Tell me what can become undone
For movement seeps its love in thee
The anchor swoons of leaded souls
In a hidden room
Last rays spent
On a rented peace
Atoning for this weary beast

Brine foams and strips the color from your face
Come wash away this ignorance
Nothing can be our unknown prophecy
Our careful retreat
Our mix of insight and thread that weaves in and out
Along the shore eroding all doubt
Has my failure to love you been loved in return?

Painted lovers unaware of their illusion
Forget their failure and fall to bed
And become the other *as* other
A cloth comes to swab their bee-stung riddled eyes
and add into the race against prayer
Has my failure to love you been loved in return?

Cotton sheath shone thin in the sun
Dries warm to cheek
Crease tucked under crease and branded underneath
From beauty forgotten to beginnings reprieved
And when prayers race against our secret addition
I will know neither heaven nor this brink
Nor think of the eternity that could subdue your newness
Wherein I remain
Uncollected among late winter tears

A recollection begun
Thoughts collect past dues
Little is done
Little as two little shoes

They barely fill them
And we go
And I follow into the inner sanctum as they fall off
And make a muted sound on marble
Hell in a host of precious claims and a Lenten hope
A little bird
A little girl
Last things are never so new
Your inverted wisdom
Your logic of perfection
Begins in each mouth

The viaticum dissolves
When swallowed
Unnoticed as it moves
How repetition soothes
Slower now
Softer now
Endure the clicking of the clock
And the tapping of the foot
The shuffling of hands and batted eyes
all fall prey to an embattled rhyme

Know that I love you
Know that in time
Words only dance here
Dance here in time

Some things fall with momentum
And others with graver notions
Save for graves that till their own
We were always held from the making of alone
Held out with the sweetness of song
Your mouth responds and hums along
And you take away what I could never convey
Splitting the infinity
That plays make believe
Plays make believe with our lives

With little lives half forgetful and gently confused
Unendingly coaxed into sunshine
And forgive my late winter tears

I will fail you if love depends upon my failure
Lean back into the inauthentic means
Forget to forgive wounded things
I am the past and past we go
Up and down
To and fro
But stay somehow in that faint and frail way
Of caring less but saying more
Find me where the torture undoes
The doe-like space behind the eyes
Remind me of those moments past
The seasoned shine of an early year

Little one
Preserve the majesty of one mortal sum
Your preservation as it was mine
From time to time
Suffer its rightness
Let it invade your senses
Give in to its taunting
Never compromised in sleep
Sail near the break
Play in its endless wake
Suffer godliness in the moment prior to the heightened failure
Hush past lust
Trust in the dead and breathe in the unsaid
Here comes Spring and all is reasonless again
Come kiss me in the light-footed way
That the holy are able to tread your surface
Confuse suffering and penance
And then return to the dance

Remorse has left us little more than cold
As laughter was prompted not cajoled

The spectators and actors all find their mark
Something warm is settling into dark
Fear to tread
For somber is a game that has left few fed
Feed and seek
Plead upon the fairytale's hands so coarse upon my cheek
This unborn act cannot service the meek

How I loved you
But had I known
That scolding time scolds alone
So alone am I
And smell of time
The Spring's soft air that sorrow defies
The wretched spinster and her sister of lies
Swiftly remove the veil of sighs

Come lie down and let your dreams prevail
Hold on to the heavy rail
And follow the dark thicket of stairs
Enter the parlor and breathe the rare
Here against care where sorrows collide
Schemes spill into empty pictures and fortify flight
They slide and crowd and crown this mayhem
Another stay for forged goodbyes

Your love has no market
And can no longer earn interest
Knowledge intersects and bruises its shelter
There is nothing more to gain
Than to bargain with what could
Or could not have been
Some things fall from gravity
Others fall into form
Make the sign of the Cross as
It finds itself and deifies all odds

The nurse of becoming has grown inhospitable
A new motivation lunges like mercury slipping on skin
Whom can I blame
I do not look the same
Eyes seared and widened in the contrast rasp
Of words against the relentless wind
Mortar wrestles its brown into the wood
And holds it down for an unseemly blend
Circles of years around years disappear
And yield to the pierce of nails
An odd unison clamped upon the bit and held
Follow the lead and trample the new seed
Knead the fragrance into the flesh
Lead us down into the lilac stench
Breach the briar of my sides and ransom its purse

Leaves in the Indian Summer
Fear for us ahead of our fear
They shake in each warm breeze
And anticipate the icy drink
That squeezes color into their veins
Sustain us in our denial
Wait a while and fall as we walk away
Staring at the stars as they play
Please fall soon
These leaves in hues
Returning to what remains
Of our intolerable ruin
Our crush of hope underfoot
Suckling on this deadened oak

Young stems
Confessionals around the bend
Leap in gravity defied
Grow soft in a mixed confide
The purpled sky revisits the flesh
As leaves dwindle down upon the breast
Nestle in the twilight of a winter's year

Dismiss even the slightest regard for what is near
Tear apart the bare
And let this fix of apathy and rage inoculate
Against the exodus that follows wherever I go
Before you go

This violence
Your blood
Does time in my mouth
Rings of my envy
Rings all about
All the children come running out
Time to go home
Time for the day's lessons to be done
Their due has been spent on a cackling fool
Clutching the thread between the leavened and the dead
Pressing it until it sponges blood within the mouth
The egg and the matter on which we feed and upon
Lost charity severed by the violence of its own extension
Calls to faith
And calls for hope
What foolish anthems will it sing to bring the little ones home again?

I would give you my undivided regret
But that takes flesh and bones
And bodily souls
And soiled hands
And hills to scavenge
And scavengers to chase
And lakes we jumped in with hearts beating
Now dried and done
I am the misfortunate compromise to outwit time
I have one promise
One promise for the bones
Confuse my dust with yours

Forgotten love leers past the penance of my yearning fears
It breathes upon my nape

Noose clutched upon the gaping absence of my sorrow
Confessions ever compromised
Holding back for the tears of tomorrow

Bid me ignorance in my time
Let me think it is dripping golden plumes from gravity's eternal tune
You are once again like amber warmed between my finger and thumb
When brevity was our only evening confidant
And we had the leisure to be despondent

Once in the vast labyrinth of time
We danced and returned
And discerned our mischief in a smile
Resistance riled a wild response crashing like lightning destroying the
    same
        Our little game
        Our grand ride at immortality
Sides run with honey and water
Blood the most certain of need-loves
Guarantees the undone
And waters the pastures across my tongue
Images collect like sap binding these abstractions
Its perfume is hideously beautiful
It is death with endless movement

I pry into half prayers bitten through half truths
I am fattened on the prospect of my own demise
Surprised at the torturous way that love confides
Exhaustion is a moment that cannot be hushed
It seeps its love in me against all odds
Its toxin of surrender cushions all pleas
I have fallen asleep under the middle tree
so disinterested am I
That I never recognized its majestic protection

In the magic of the dark and deep wood
Her subtle hold found release
And left me a labyrinth to tame

Racked with certitude and shame
Those vessels of mine would no longer resist
I insist I can live while bleeding thee out

There was once a porous stone for time's kindnesses to maim
Its cancerous redemption spread the same
The same thoughts
The same memories
That same shirt
A terrible shirt
No—it was a lovely shirt
Orange checkers worn proud and thoroughly grey
Once or twice in time one remarks how easy it is to pray
Knees were built for kneelers
And words for the chasm
Fingers built for the fold
Eyes built for thy penitent stares

Rather than wait for the solemnity
Between the lashings and the tree
And as I pulled and fashioned and sharpened loss into lances
You were never less than Good
What inescapable matter you are!
Your wisdom carnal and incarnate
A preserved nature
A pulp
A soft tissue extending space
Your nature reserved for death was mine to come
In these recesses I became momentum

God release me from the things neither wanted nor hid
I want them more with every moment
With every pulse that bribes

Time has come for you
To pierce my sides
In the nightingale's song
I will still love you

Your wings in your hands
Do not be afraid of suffering
You are only right when you suffer
Do not fear the way in which gravity
Cannot speed the honeybee to the flower
Nor the way it kisses you goodbye

Presence rages against its own embrace
And the hum of the wood neither endures
Nor recants for you as it should
As it must for two creatures of confused boundaries

Discantus supra meum

Sing above the ground
And above the book
And above the little things found
On walks around sheltered little towns
Oh my love sing for our lost souls too lost to begin
For they alone complete their rescue missions
For they alone have nothing left to show
Slower now and softer

With you little one
I make believe and preen this sweet scented folly
Falling into the perilous pretend
I am relieved of loving what I do not know
Proffered in the next hand we go
Gamboling along the sing song night
Liminal light cast on shedding sands
Feet scurry and erase
Finger lined drawings that race along the sound
Little clams holed in against the wind
The salt and our lively assault

These things of grace
These blessings in disguise with each rise of the tide
Confound this heavy ground and pound a tendering pace

Hand after hand patterns curl around like lace
Your face wet in my hands
How I loved you so
In you I can love what I do not know
Hell hides in a single refrain
The monarchy of perfection
Of perfect seconds
Minutes
Motions
Quickened commotions
That augur the eternal in the ephemeral
And slap the tame into the temporal
Hell in a single refrain

Love and uncertainty dangle
Two souls who abate their breath
Held to the burn and then only then
Lend their form to the sight of the dawn
The night whispers to the day
And calls the evening for its yearning play

He does not cry
Tears fall in ravenous rush
His movements are enough
Limbs and bodies fall from heights unknown
The sting of adoration intoxicates the eyes
Blown sweet dust from an unknown demise
Reprise
Time spent with lovers looming over the edge to feel the breeze
Blackness seeps its hands in me
It seizes all color and is unwilling to retreat

Come lay with me upon the heavy soil
Where all grief comes to loom
With little room for roses among the white chrysanthemum

Sing for the roses that open
And drown in and for the dew

How differently they bloom
Lift their lids to what gives them sight
Blinded and divided in the nearness of the mortal touch
Hush now
Quiet now
Softer now
This empty room
Its single light

Yours is the lost bride who blushed the winter's rose
She the gilded summer where all things dance
Even in memory they still dance
Unknown prayers made lame in actions recalled
Never recollect only stall
Around these shards.
If you find the one graceful like petals
You have found the one who can cut them all

But such touch cannot be
She peers from the space between nowhere and the sea
Imparting and bringing one severely close
Nearer still and farther out
Hollow hold of memory bites back its vellum tears
Seasons come shined and dulled
Seeds collected in a line
Find place in the tender soil
Heavy is this mind that grows old
But will it grow kind?

Bleeding against the sacraments of the home
Communion alone
Desires to place your body
Among the little things that press their weight like stones
Passion opens and drowns
Brown comes to mingle in the red
Colors so simple we are led
Up ahead I heed your words
Their nectar upon my forehead

You beg for caution against the curiosity of my waking sight
My flight from form
Rhythm quickens upon the lips to trace the place
Where little fingers quiet thee in thy Grace
And that is why I sleep
You hush me gently and tell me not to be afraid
Of a fear that is growing grandly all the time
Your grace is silent but it is there
It is silent but it is there
Repeating your cause
my cause in yours
Silent but there

Razors scout their way through my voice
The only sounds left
Are not the ones I need
The lilac litany answers with its first snap
Bones brittle form a trap
This body
This blood
There is no escape into the white or even the cream
Lines retract their abstractions and force flesh upon the ream

Prayers cease into prayers turned in against the tongue
All wants want to be undone

The long night gathers its folds like an old dressing gown
collected and positioned for lying down
Incantations recant and break into autumn spells
Bend down and collect your sash
The reign of a livid remorse has just begun

This soft cheek does not wither in the frost
Only blushes in its first winter,
It knows no uncertainty that comes from mixtures such as these
Salts to preserve and tears to appease
The majesty of their tragic scold
She blossoms in the prospect of the fold

My reckless confidant
My inverted wisdom
I have no answer for you but the burn
Quiet now
Softer now
Wrest tenderness from its hidden pace

I must confess restless things
Know little equivalency
When tempted with the unveiled matter of the ghost
And what can overthrow and receive your countenance
But one full of repose

Life among relics is a quiet parade of faded things
The insides of lace lined linen
Stained with holy water and the oil of sniffled tears
Tried and hushed his hesitant failing
And failed with Beauty again and again

SED CONTRA: VIA NEGATIVA

"That which is to be hath already been . . . "

Yours is a strange resolve dried and reared
A treaty of good deeds
Rallying content in unreasoning dreams
Dappled with curling shadows
Like silkworms through cloth blotted on sacred things
Shapes with presence enough to flood for sleep
Never enough substance to configure form
In and through and along their lines and rows
You see what can belong is tinged with the same force
That ceases movement
And seizes our soured frames from peering longer than before

Your movement seeps its love in me
But it cannot swab the ink from my eyes
Tranquility unrequited in the waking memory

You grow old with age
Huddled into the frame twice the rate as I
Keep this brooding hum close to my sides
Ease this fear growing greatly all the time
Save me from this grave and uneven notion
That my youth was spent in lacking
Preserve me from the way you bend
I cannot be so brave
I cannot crave the ways of surrender

Turn on turn
Nullity reforms and finds
Something other to deform
Come mingle in the mix and maze of hands
Movement's maddening play runs up and down my sides
Prompting flight

What kind of time hides in your flesh?
Hush this mesh of wings
I will not relent

The cliffs are clay and rub up against us
Your words press their fingers inside my throat
The obscene dissonance curdles the air
You've turned me out
My God my God have you forsaken all your care?

My distance growls a countenance for its own emptiness
Wrap around and drag us down into the resin bend
Our company reeks of honeybees and flies
Trapped too in the rhythmic display of the thread we lay
Hips in sway
Insistent and found
And what alone can turn us away
From this sight of bodies frozen in play
Movements held longer than before
All control is left to courage

Worthless care is all I have
It causes more hope than despair
Its roads sink into a rudder gray
Its miles confounded are pounded numb
This maze loops around finger and thumb
A passage sung for forgotten souls
In a forgotten Mass swells with unabated fury
And summons another rung
Worthless care is all that you bore
It caused more upon more
A generation in decay

The little novitiate comes down
With pearl beads and wood ones too
Down to drown the little eyelets of despair
Precipitation dares to run against caution
Fallen forth in the splendor of exhaustion

Tiny ants march along the jaw-line curve
Little death is free for speed
The bee's movement terrifyingly
Works its math in me
Thoughtless blood and time for all time
Make the sign of the cross
It defies all odds

Fluids engage your futility and refuse the call
Left in madness and torn asunder
Wondering why all first things are left in slumber
Curiosity knows no omission
Oh but how it wells!

Let it all go forth and fall
Like the sound of bells
Come gleam
Streaming in the viscosity that only the shape of lips can make
Draining in the mouth
Welling in the tongue
This likened sustenance of my youth undone.

Where is the Virgin who cradles a sweet frame
With hollowness years could never contain
Brush it all away
All things decay
No matter which way
We forgive or pray to be forgiven

Forgive me
Forgive me for having my hand
In the imitation of your Grace

How far should one extend in circumstance
Stigmatized by the futility
That turns the dancer to an even stance
I gasp upon this brace
Held up in mortality

Uneven
Shaking and breaching all divide

What more will cordon this regret
And bring the hearth into home
We go in memory and in lack
Let me sew these wings upon your back
Find the bruises in my kiss
Ignore their little hiss
Smother the blinding fury of the glow
Summering bride where did you go?

Your hold is a stow away salve
Soothing and salvaging me
And every creature has a prior tincture to show
That it has flown past anticipation
And lingers low in recollection

What color has love dappled you my maudlin love?

Stay little one
For the violet haze
At the end of the blue
Need not be seen
For these seeds in our skin have broken through
And their growth will do our bidding
In all the resplendent shades from heather to gray

Act out the greatest play
Revisit the nearness of every passing threat
One hand clutched in death-like stance
The other pummeling into chance
A steady soil is leaded with grief in chase
Heavy lids attempt to fill the breach of space
Brief motivations bound our wrists
Exhaustion subdues and then resists
I can taste you still when the gleam is gone
Pound this chest and let all haunting transpire

I have known no such longing as not to be free
I am learning to be frightened of all things
Innocence betrays kindness for a fixed fee
It wraps its tendons completely patterned after you
I can only stay here
My movement is limited unlike my fear
This presentiment-need ignites the trees
Summer bleeds into an autumn freeze
Wax hardens and thickens into blisters
Seize this unrepeatability and try again
To find the sacred things
Crush the cold and brush away the folded leaves
And their somber code
Tapping imperceptibly upon the virgin snow

Do not pause for love as I pause
I watched you as you spoke so mildly
How movement slid across the tongue
To produce such reasonless beauty
Pull me in to the splendid ways
That remorse lays its ground
For future workings upon the back

Little death
Straighten your limbs and try again
And press your hands to the briar at my sides
Confuse the storm with heavenly and fevered fingers
Squeeze doubt with life
This magic under form

Sounds of a floating choir remove the dissonance
Their insistence spills into perfect pitch
Notes hang like children upon the marrow of this divide
And produce silence denied
The movement of bodies beasts and stars
Ease bodies just like ours
Forgive me for following blindly behind
Your sides are just like mine

Cold to sound still warm to touch
But things can change in our ravenous clutch

There is nothing more to throw
Sacred things have settled below
Watch the actors pivot and bow
Watch how fate escapes with the swollen rain
We strangers staring through a window pane
Saturated and twisted lane
Tree lines to erase train lines
Too many solid things weathered to rust
Pummeling fists interrogate the dust
And pelt the water's edge
Hell becomes the holy in a single refrain

I have faith
But you must speak calmly
These words have yet to take hold
All that remains are sweet presses lingering softly
In the mist of fine fallen ribbons so near

I would give you my youth preserved in prayer
Thrown with the certitude of twilight's watchful stare
Be relieved all color has faded
Trade your sight for the thought of night
There is more beauty to seek
Than all birds find
Peering their yellowed brims
In crevices next to the medicine of sin.

I cannot lie
I watched you play along the lines and rows
I think I can hold you from the making of alone

The tendered soil shows
More than exhaustion works its math in me
I have withered well for you
Vespers sanctify your newly forged sides

I am hoping repentance undoes the agony of repetition
I pray to ease you of your curiosity
Such waters to haunt

All things are dust in my pockets and in my shoes
Little girls in dresses with Sunday blooms in tiny hands
Walking behind flows a trail of sugar and sand
Like breadcrumbs for the little ones
Who need to learn how to return home

Do not pick me up
Leave me be
Let him sleep
Let him not know the hour's longing
And filled with anticipation
Let me ease you
Let me say
That it was okay to shy away
From the brilliance that fades
The tincture of the roses and the blessed
It leaves its song in its passing flesh

I will sing to you softly

Please play here in the damp leaves
That makes no crush of hope underfoot
Let your words slow to the pit patter of little toes
Ribs joined with our rosin are caged by frail hands
Free to expand from lovers to damned
The convocation of two souls holds no reflection
Apart from their shared shape
No action
Nor word
Nor treason
Could engage this loss
Find me outside the faith begging for its sacred drape
Relieve me of this end that only rage can endure

I have no fear of being trampled
I will not relent
Forget everything above nature
Of time and eternity
And consciousness and perdurance
Consciousness is always consciousness of
That shabby separation
Another hermit and his caravan
Little crabs scurry among every morsel of sand
Shells so unfixed
Two of them dot and bolt in perfect commitment
Commuting our sentiments

Do not wager my plea
Even if it is there
I am always here
Do not bring me around
Or wash me of this clay
Wax and caked fibers suppress my chest
I hold you with fear
The only way you allow me to hold you near
My eyes peer at the ceiling
Yours have the sky

Come tell me of the crestfallen gestures lovers make
When their hold is told not to take
My love is thawing lack
And there are such things
That can only linger between two mortalities
Like lashings they linger
Your presence is revealed
And removes itself from the guise hook

Elements caught in the mouths of myths with wings
Born from sand and other such things
Fall on ashes crisped with frost and bid thee sleep
Come home follow the sugar in the frost
Sweet nothings lull the lost through the night

Sugarplum purpled skin
Stretched fingers across the arrow's base
Sleep do not hesitate for all first things are left in slumber

Flooded plums
Sweet to taste
Devouring every curve
Love conditioned and conscribed
Only mouth the word and I shall be healed

RESPONDEO DICENDUM: LONGIOR VIA

"And God requires that which is past."

It is always so for those solemn souls
Where in longing one can only know
The severance on the tip of tongue
Do not go
Sweet suffering soul
Even if the mountains hushed in white
Show the first scars of green
Things can lean and bend and take your shape

What could be
And what still remains
If it is stilled of its trembling
All memory pauses in the nearness of an unshared touch
Toughened tallow along the cusp rushes towards the bright
And presses its pale into the last silhouettes of Grace
Our foolish things
Our piano chimes
Our strawberries and sunburns
You never knew love felt so like fear

Your ghost writhes
The summer's heat pries ice into lips and chides
There is nothing left that does not remind
I've swept back and forth through hair and hands
I've followed the shapes lovers make
This wake is worn thin of its ether lace
The darkened love of my faith is held in hands that taper excess
And fall like sirens to their sides

God forgive me my curiosity
Your constant trail is nowhere to be found
The echoes behind the stage of our shared nature fail to resound

Our vast entanglement of time never missed nor stalled
Now it is gone
Patterns after patterns
After possibility have called for reality to emerge
Not one word spans nor withstands its own stoning
As gravity groans

Last call recognitions purge movement
A strange wetness begins to surge
Our grand confrontation
Our last anticipation
The first sting of salt water is carried into the hills
It conjures the sweet nothing of sublimation but nothing of sin
Such brevity in spring
How many confessions around the bend will weigh an even end
And atone for these martyred hopes having gone too far
After actions after patterns after you

Viscerate these crowds of grief and come alone

When the prescient end is known
It knows not what to suffer and then suffers through all things
In the fortitude and strength of its circumstance
Lies brevity gnawing at your sides bitten clear to its source
In there lies the brooding hum for which interest was lost and found
Lost and then found
Wrap around and suffocate without notice
Round out this day with senseless remorse
Senses without remorse
And pray there is no parity set in this hanging threat
For which we seek to divide the tendered skin
From the taciturn sky

I have not suffered your love enough to love thee in return
My God, My God deliver me from this flesh folded upon flesh precipice of
  prayer

These are but names and you are dying still
Placed once upon a time in a line
He pays no mind to the little ones
Sprouting a trail between winter and time
For they mimic the great and elusive beast
Who rang mortality through you
And for him there can be no parity in this hanging threat
When bringing forth a tender skin to hasten the night

My little one what have you done?
I've hushed my lips in the sugar and the frost
I have not suffered your love enough to love thee in return
My God finish it off and forsake me
For I will take it all
From penance to wrath
I will take all and take it back to the ground

My child
My love you are the dying
Relent and fall asleep in our autumn sin
Your unhappiness is forgiven

We are criminals and faith is our crime
Do not disbelieve these are the flights I require
Pressed in cadence to the grate
Fate's rigid enterprise vacates the eyes
Swabs with little flies and never needs your love to conspire

The freedom to lay cold to the ground is met with a challenge
to kill the underlying cause of your demise
for perfection is in the way
one loves in the image of the divine

We have little time
Just like you little one
Beg for distractions
Speak more smile and breathe
Kiss me tenderly and leave me for sleep

If I wake
Hold me closer than the memory of the summering bride
Dancing into one and one part
These parts collect and rear their little heads
Its growing fear gnaws at the nape but also at the noose
They have asked to take it all away
But I prefer to stay

The unhappiness of forgiven sins
Is a strange resolve
Its poetry its mist hovers alongside tears too ashamed to fall
Too weak to retreat

Let me stay
A pale flower pulled away
A tear of Christ
A stain on a stain
Let me stay here
Where there are no petals underfoot

Thy penitent hold knows no agony of his longing
That is mine for you my child
Be faithful
You are my little one of sums never undone
You know not what remains except this quiet strange
Folded into your sides as they are mine
Lanced with the lashings of all time
You are the press of pallor upon your kind
I shall deliver you in time

Incantations invoke an early spring
On mouths of myths and other nameless things
Reprieved of the fallen clenched folly of another
Though never absolved of wanting its cover
You sprung the ways in which one can love
And placated the kiss of youth with the risk to soothe
Sun drenches the sand and rigors the plum vine

Courage cannot control its ecstasy lined
Trace the insteps and the thighs
And lead us to the woven clue

The father felt the heave of two as one
The belly rises one last great gasp
Towards Heaven's lilac sighs
Dreams level and fall forth
But first with spews and flames of ashen over gold
The crimson snow
These are the ways the gods show
They are little children of little men
Never mending nor minding their happy end

I have lost the trail in the winter's snow
Breadcrumbs brushed aside from mouth and hand
Become a thrush of lines undone and words unsaid
Bristling unrecognizable underneath the skin
My failsafe cloth blotted the past intangibility that nears
A salt worn thin on stone in mutual measure
And you
You have consumed every visitation of memory
Save how nature re-positions itself for another cast of indifference

Vanquish this crown of relief and come home

Prayers ravaged with age dig to preserve the eternal
To save this passing moment
Its readymade lacuna
Already a handful of dust
Another sacred line finds homage in the basement of Being
Redeem its value and eulogize this half dead corpse
Its succor is its repetition
Its unfaithful recollection

I have begged for those low slung craters
Scant of dwelling
To bed my rapture in a deep and unholy silence

Throbbing into sensation and past every motivation
I know what can become undone
Your remains never remain the same
There is no laughter in the upstairs room
We have all been made lame

The gentle chain that lays in wait
Has been all too kind to remind
Tears link and braise the cheek
Falling without reason
Devouring all thought in a single stream
For lines into rows
For miles and miles
One image remains

Pray for me Mary Mother of God
Pray for this bent over and broken casted soul
Copper iron and older than I

Pray for the little ones with sums undone

Broken bread over broken folly
Love is ruthless and selfless
The great paradox
Bewildered and dead
You said
Consummatum est

Love my love
Is nothing more nor nothing less than
                              Consummatum est
Selfless and ruthless you are
Forgiving as autumn frost you are

One bread one Flesh
One wine one Blood
        In and through the aisles of time

Come home
Rain falls soft
Hardening hands fold
Bite back your ambushed tears and forgive me
Lay your weight on me and forgive me
Soothe this savagery and forgive me
I cannot wait forgive me
I lay in wait forgive me

Tears crashing like lightning to soothe the same
The same agony of repetition
My prayers find words only for the moment
Loving and relentless God forgive me

Viscerate these crowds of grief and come alone

Remain faithful to the pulse that bribes as it scavenges
Ransom all your kindness
And suffer what is done
A pure sound runs its fingers over my eyes
And threatens to love me in turn
My failure to love you is loved in return
I have not suffered your love enough to love thee in return

My God My God deliver me from this flesh folded upon flesh precipice of
   prayer

Love is a strange sanctification
A stranger retrodiction
Love is a strange inculcation
An even stranger calculation
Forget words
Forget time
Expire the abbreviations between the surface and the shine
Myth ravages as it impels its balm into my chest
Its body of art
Its grafted stare
You alone ingrain fingers to the wood

And relieve the languid sin

I am not worthy that you should enter under my roof
But only say the word

Word for souls to be healed
Word to stain and brave remain
My unhappiness clamors outside the begotten
And finds itself forgiven
Fallow hopes become claret lines draping chrism and stone
A mortal God carved out of the rigor
Discloses himself on your face
Tattered edges sink into lips and begin to feed
A coupling felt bead after bead
A quivering waltz leads beyond the loving smear
Of blood and fear where faith is repaired

In our rhythmic decay
This forgotten God
Stretches every tendon in our hands
Into the place of sacred things
On stone
On wood
On chest
On lines that cross and never divide
Come home
Follow the sugar and the frost

Vanquish this crown of relief and come home

Moments tender for presence
Time to invoke shape
Shade for its own embrace
I have raced against the sun and let all warmth
Become an oil to soothe the chase
Chasten me with the fear curled in my spine
Show me it is not an evil far too confined
I climb towards the God unknown

Who eases every fleck of skin before falling forth
At the prospect of life anew
I have known no such fear as this easing nearness
Besieged by nothing and out of nothing
Only say the word

One Word and one image remain
One sacrifice to stain and free
Follow the agony of the rose
Upon the head and then the chest
two fingers end and dent a place beneath bone
Into the soft pit curve of little shoulders
One after one
Come home
And return the loving spell of blood and time
Pressed upon our kind
Faithful things
Foolish things
Such spoken things have frayed far into the below

In the ended prayer
Somber as evening frost
In the first night
A novitiate in grief
Sings the gentle retreat

Ended prayers
Prayers forgotten
Ended hopes
Hopes forgotten

To the ends
To the ends of the earth that span across your face
And wet your cheek
As it was mine

Forgiving as autumn frost
You are

My God why have you given this to me?
This incomprehensible beauty
This perfection of joy round and full
Why have you not forsaken me
Your lowly and unfaithful servant?
In this the only and undone act
A prayer of thanksgiving
For these things too perfect to hold
For such beautiful things
I know not how to give over
Under bread and flesh
On blood
Through the ultimate grace
A sacrifice made

Sing to these dying gods my dying God
Call home these sirens of despair
Lilting in the verses of receding waves
Tumbling in your flesh
For you alone can cross the infinite endings
And bring thyself from the threshold of home into home

www.ingramcontent.com/pod-product-compliance
Lightning Source LLC
Chambersburg PA
CBHW060347090426
42734CB00011B/2061